Donald Justice

in conversation with

Philip Hoy

Donald Justice

in conversation with

Philip Hoy

BETWEEN THE LINES BTL BETWEEN THE LINES

First published in 2001 by

BETWEEN THE LINES **BTL** BETWEEN THE LINES

9 Woodstock Road
London N4 3ET
UK

T : +44 (0)20 8374 5526 F : +44 (0)20 8374 5736 E-mail : btluk@aol.com
Website: http://www.interviews-with-poets.com

A CIP catalogue record for this book
is available from the British Library

Paperback Edition
ISBN 0 9532841 9 0

Hardback Limited Signed Edition
ISBN 1 903291 01 1

Design: Philip Hoy

Paperback edition printed and bound by George Over Limited,
Somers Road, Rugby CV22 7DH.

Hardback Edition printed by George Over Limited
and bound by Blissetts Bookbinders, Roslin Road, London, W3 8DH

BTL publishes unusually wide-ranging and unusually deep-going interviews with some of today's most accomplished poets.

Some would deny that any useful purpose is served by putting to a writer questions which are not answered by his or her books. For them, what Yeats called 'the bundle of accident and incoherence that sits down to breakfast' is best left alone, not asked to interrupt its cornflakes, or to set aside its morning paper, while someone with a tape recorder inquires about its life, habits and attitudes.

If we do not share this view, it is not because we endorse Sainte-Beuve's dictum, *tel arbre, tel fruit* — *as the tree, so the fruit* — but because we understand what Geoffrey Braithwaite was getting at when the author of *Flaubert's Parrot* had him say:

> 'But if you love a writer, if you depend upon the drip-feed of his intelligence, if you want to pursue him and find him — despite edicts to the contrary — then it's impossible to know too much.'

The first eight volumes, featuring W.D. Snodgrass, Michael Hamburger, Anthony Thwaite, Anthony Hecht, Donald Hall, Thom Gunn, Richard Wilbur, and Seamus Heaney, respectively, are already available; others now being prepared will feature Ian Hamilton, Charles Simic, Paul Muldoon, Hans Magnus Enzensberger, and Peter Porter (Further details are given overleaf.)

As well as the interview, each volume contains a sketch of the poet's life and career, a comprehensive bibliography, archival information, and a representative selection of quotations from the poet's critics and reviewers. It is hoped that the results will be of interest to the lay reader and specialist alike.

— OTHER VOLUMES FROM BTL —

— FORTHCOMING —

CONTENTS

ACKNOWLEDGEMENTS

The editors would like to thank the following people for their help in producing this book: Danny Gillane (for the comprehensive bibliography to be found on pages 97-118), Nathaniel Justice (for permission to use the photograph of Donald Justice which appears on the cover of this book and on page 10), Jim Reidel (for allowing us to read in manuscript parts of his forthcoming biography, *Vanishing Act: The Life and Art of Weldon Kees*), Tim Murray (Head of the Special Collections Department in the University of Delaware Library, who supplied copies of unpublished documents in the Justice archive), and David Hamilton and Michelle Giguere (respectively editor of *The Iowa Review* and assistant editor of *The Antioch Review*, who helped us to trace items that had appeared in their pages).

We should also like to acknowledge a debt to Dana Gioia and William Logan, the editors of *Certain Solitudes: On the Poetry of Donald Justice,* a book whose essays, reviews, memoirs and interview proved invaluable in the preparation of this volume.

Finally, we should like to express our gratitude to Donald Justice himself, for having given us permission to print the uncollected poems, the linocuts, and the extracts from his musical scores which appear on pages 87-90, 91-94 and 95-96, respectively, as well as for his hard work in ensuring our bibliography's completeness.

Donald Justice

Photograph courtesy of
Nathaniel Justice

A NOTE ON DONALD JUSTICE

Donald Justice was born in Miami, Florida, on August 12th 1925, the only child of Vasco and Mary Ethel Justice (née Cook).

Justice attended Allapattah Elementary School, Andrew Jackson High School and the Senior High School in Miami. Then, in the autumn of 1942, he enrolled for a BA in Music at the University of Miami, where he studied for a time with the composer Carl Ruggles. At a certain point, however, Justice decided that he might have more talent as a writer than a composer, and when he took his degree, in 1945, it was not in Music but English.

After a year spent working at odd jobs in New York, Justice entered the University of North Carolina – the University of North Carolina, Chapel Hill, as it is now known – to study for an MA. There he got to know a number of other people who would go on to make their mark as writers, amongst them the novelist Richard Stern, the poet Edgar Bowers, and the short story writer, Jean Ross, whom he married in 1947, the year he took his MA.

Justice accepted a one-year appointment instructing in English at the University of Miami. Then, with the encouragement of Edgar Bowers, who had gone there the year before, he took up the offer of a place to study for a PhD at Stanford University in California, where he hoped to work under the supervision of Yvor Winters. Unfortunately, the head of department refused to allow this, and, mindful of Justice's teaching load, insisted that he took only one course per semester, thereby condemning him to very slow progress. Frustrated, Justice left Stanford and went back to Florida, where he resumed the life of an instructor at the University of Miami.

Early in 1951, the Pandanus Press published a small chapbook of Justice's work, *The Old Bachelor and Other Poems.* But if the occasion was cause for celebration, it will have been overshadowed by the announcement that the university was letting all of its English instructors go.

Out of work, and unsure what to do next, Justice acted on the advice of friends and applied to study for the PhD in Creative Writing being offered by the Iowa Writer's Workshop, the oldest institution of its kind in America, founded by Paul Engle in 1937. His application was successful, and in the spring of 1952 Justice joined one of the most distinguished classes ever to pass through the Workshop, his fellow students including Jane

Cooper, Henri Coulette, Robert Dana, William Dickey, Philip Levine, W.D. Snodgrass and William Stafford.

In the spring of 1954, just two years after his arrival, Justice obtained his PhD, and was promptly awarded a Rockefeller Foundation Fellowship in poetry, which made it possible for him to travel to Europe for the first time. After his return, he spent two years as an assistant professor, one at the University of Missouri at Columbia, the other at Hamline University, St Paul, Minnesota. Then, in 1957, he went back to the Iowa Writers' Workshop, where he had agreed to take over some of his teaching while Engle was away on leave. This was to have been a temporary appointment, but when Engle returned, he was asked to stay on, and he remained at the Workshop for over ten years.

Justice had been publishing poems in many of the country's leading journals – amongst them, *Poetry, The New Yorker, Harper's, The Hudson Review,* and *The Paris Review* – and he had been publishing short stories as well – two had been included in O. Henry Prize Stories annual collections – but it wasn't until 1960, when he was thirty-five years old, that Wesleyan University Press published his first full collection, *The Summer Anniversaries.* It was very well received: 'Mr Justice is an accomplished writer,' wrote Howard Nemerov, 'whose skill is consistently subordinated to an attitude at once serious and unpretentious. Although his manner is not yet fully disengaged from that of certain modern masters, whom he occasionally echoes, his own way of doing things does in general come through, a voice distinct although very quiet, in poems that are delicate and brave among their nostalgias.' In competition with books submitted by forty-seven other publishers, *The Summer Anniversaries* was chosen by the Academy of American Poets as the Lamont Poetry Selection for 1959.

Two small press publications came out in the next few years – *A Local Storm* in 1963 and *Three Poems* in 1966 – and so did two edited volumes – *The Collected Poems of Weldon Kees* in 1960 and *Contemporary French Poetry* in 1965 – and then, in 1967, the year he left the Iowa Writers' Workshop, Justice's second full collection was published. *Night Light* was a very different book from its predecessor, but although it drew some negative reviews – William H. Pritchard summed up his reaction by saying that the book was 'almost wholly about literature, often not very exciting literature' – and some of the positive reviews were lazily formulated, Justice will have found the general tenor of the pieces reassuring: 'This is a book to be grateful for,' wrote one reviewer, and most of the others were clearly in agreement.

Justice left the Iowa Writers' Workshop in order to take up an Associate

Professorship at Syracuse University in New York. The following year – a year in which he was awarded a National Endowment for the Arts fellowship in poetry, and gave the Elliston lectures at the University of Cincinnati – he was appointed full professor. However, Justice remained at Syracuse University for only three years, accepting a one-year appointment at the University of California at Irvine in 1970, and then, in the autumn of 1971, going back for a third time to Iowa.

Two more small press publications came out in the early 1970s – *Sixteen Poems* in 1970 and *From a Notebook* in 1972. These were followed by Justice's third full collection, *Departures*, which was published in 1973, and was another critical success. Irvin Ehrenpreis described its author as a 'profoundly gifted' poet. Richard Howard was no less enthusiastic: '[T]his little book [contains] some of the most assured, elegant and heartbreaking ... verse in our literature so far.' *Departures* was nominated for the 1973 National Book Award.

Justice's *Selected Poems* was published in 1979, and its jacket bore a ringing endorsement from Anthony Hecht: 'Many admiring poets and a few perceptive critics (Paul Fussell, Jr among them) have paid careful, even studious attention to Donald Justice's poetic skill, which seems able to accomplish anything with an ease that would be almost swagger if it were not so modest of intention. He is, among other things, the supreme heir of Wallace Stevens. His brilliance is never at the service merely of flash and display; it is always subservient to experienced truth, to accuracy, to Justice, the ancient virtue as well as the personal signature. He is one of our finest poets.' Not all of the reviewers were so well-disposed, however. Calvin Bedient described Justice as 'an uncertain talent that has not been turned to much account'; Gerald Burns said that the volume 'reads like a very thin Tennessee Williams'; and Alan Hollinghurst said that the poems, 'formal but fatigués ... create the impression of getting great job satisfaction without actually doing much work.' Still, those who felt like Bedient, Burns and Hollinghurst were in a small minority, and Justice's *Selected Poems* was awarded the Pulitzer Prize for poetry in 1980.

In 1982 Justice returned to the state of his birth to take up a professorship at the University of Florida, Gainsville. Two years later he published *Platonic Scripts,* which gathered a number of his critical essays and a handful of the interviews he had given since the mid-1960s. Then, in 1987, he published his next full collection, *The Sunset Maker,* a book whose contents were well described by his old friend Richard Stern in a review for *The Chicago Tribune*: 'Poems built so finely out of such intricate emotional music shift in the mind from reading. They are the products, if not the barometer, of an extraordinary temperament coupled with enormous verbal and rhythmic skill. No poem here could have been written by anyone but Donald Justice. This is his world, faintly tropical, faintly melancholy, musical, affectionate, a fixity of evanescence. Beautiful as little else.'

In 1991, by which time he had written the libretto for Edwin London's opera, *The Death of Lincoln*, and had co-edited *The Collected Poems of Henri Coulette*, Justice was awarded the Bollingen Prize, in recognition of a lifetime's achievement in poetry.

The following year, disenchanted with Florida, and disaffected with the university, Justice retired and moved back to Iowa City. Since then, he has published a number of books: *A Donald Justice Reader* (containing poems, a memoir, short stories and critical essays) appeared in 1992, *New and Selected Poems* and *Banjo Dog* in 1995, *Oblivion* (containing critical essays, appreciations and extracts from notebooks) and *Orpheus Hesitated Beside the Black River* (an English version of his *New and Selected Poems*) in 1998. He has also co-edited *The Comma After Love: Selected Poems of Raeburn Miller* (1994) and Joe Bolton's *The Last Nostalgia: Poems 1982-1990* (1999).

In 1997, Justice was elected a chancellor of the Academy of American Poets. He and his wife still live in Iowa City. They have one son, Nathaniel, who was born in 1961.

A Note on Philip Hoy

Philip Hoy was born in London in 1952, and educated at the Universities of York and Leeds. He has a PhD in Philosophy, a subject he taught for many years, here in the UK and overseas. His most recent publications are *W.D. Snodgrass in Conversation with Philip Hoy* (BTL, 1998) and *Anthony Hecht in Conversation with Philip Hoy* (BTL, 1999, 2001). He lives in north London with the architect Evelina Francia.

THE CONVERSATION

In November 2000, Donald Justice was sent a list of more than one hundred questions. His answers to these questions were received in four instalments, the first arriving in January, and the last in March, 2001. Thirty or so supplementary questions were sent in April, and the poet's answers to these were received a month later.

You were born in Miami, Florida, but your parents weren't from there origi-nally, as I understand it. They'd moved there as part of the 1920s land boom.

My parents were from south Georgia, a region of villages and small farms. After World War I, in which he had served with the Allied Expeditionary Force, my father seems to have drifted southward through the small towns of north Florida, working at various jobs, picking up the elements of carpentry, the trade he would follow for the rest of his life. He ended up in Miami, which was humming then with all the possibilities of a new frontier, much new construction, and newcomers arriving daily, many of them, like my parents, from the lower South. Indeed, if you stopped by the downtown post office, you were likely to find, seated on the broad neo-classical steps of the building, sunning themselves, people from your own part of the world, peo-ple you might know or who would know relatives of yours. This was exactly how my mother's brother, Ralph, when he showed up in Miami, got the address of my parents, from some Thomas County acquaintance sitting there on the steps. In the early Twenties this would have been. My father had returned to Georgia briefly to marry my mother, and the two of them had what must have seemed an epic honeymoon trip down the east coast of Florida. The trip took three days, sometimes over one-lane roads, not yet paved, fording streams on plank bridges, and so on. Hard to conceive, look-ing backward from Florida as it is now. I am pretty sure they found it excit-ing; they spoke of it for years afterward. And a city like the just then booming city of Miami must have been exciting for them – everything new and very bright. Also – and this was the really important thing – it was possible to make a decent living there. The hurricane of 1926 proved devastating, though. The land boom ended all at once with that – and the depression started three years early in Miami. I remember still the day my father came home unex-pectedly at noon – he had been out that morning searching for a job, as he had been for weeks, perhaps months – to announce that he had with great good luck found something, a job which promised steady employment for years to come. That morning I had watched my mother packing my father's suitcase – he was about to head out to Texas, where he had heard there was work. Now we could stay in Miami, and that very job was to last until World War II, so that all through the worst years of the depression we enjoyed a

17

steady if modest income.

Can you tell us more about your parents – their educational backgrounds, and so on?

My father, who had been born in a very small settlement called Pansey, in Alabama, had had three years of school in a rural schoolhouse near the family farm in Tifton, Georgia. My mother had had eleven years of school – I don't remember now if she had graduated from her home town high school in Boston, Georgia, or not. I think not. But she had had more of what were called advantages than my father – and these included piano lessons on the same upright I learned to play on myself, and which lasted as the family piano into the Sixties. (It was almost always out of tune, persistently a half-tone flat, and I remember still the special plangency of two or three of its notes, particularly the B just below middle C – a sound I found strangely beautiful.)

My father worked hard all his life and liked the work, liked nothing better, I think. Two months after retiring he died. Some of his friends believed that it was stopping work that killed him. One of my childhood memories of him is of lying in bed as I recuperated from the osteomyelitis that knocked me out of school for a year and, as darkness fell, hearing a hammer pounding away nearby and suddenly realizing that this was my father, working on the house he was building, almost single-handedly, on a neighbouring lot, hoping for enough profit to take care of my large medical expenses. He had already worked a full day at his regular job; this was extra.

My mother was more sociable, more gregarious, ever 'on the go', as she sometimes put it.

Did religion play an important part in the life of your family? You were raised a Southern Baptist, I know.

My mother was the only regular churchgoer in her family or my father's, though my father allowed himself to be dragged along pretty often, and I did not really know how to get out of it myself, or out of the dreary hour of Sunday school which preceded the morning sermon. We were all of us Southern Baptists without question, my cousins, my uncles and aunts, everyone; it was just that most of them were only rarely to be found inside a church. For me the worst times came during the revival meetings, when souls were publicly saved, or else during the 'fire and brimstone' sermons of some of the preachers, who had a certain vaudevillian talent admired by my mother. By the age of ten or eleven I did learn how to avoid some of all this: in the course of a particularly fiery sermon my nose would suddenly begin to bleed, and I would be permitted to take refuge in the quiet darkness of our parked car, out of range of the preacher's excited voice. This never failed to cure my nosebleed.

Did you have any brothers or sisters, or were you an only child?

I was an only child, and as such I was spoiled, especially by my mother, who gave me the sense early on that what I did I could and should do well, the sense also that we were as good as anyone and ought *never* to forget that. Other poor families of our acquaintance were touched by just such a pride, I think, and were certainly none the worse for it.

Did your parents read much?

Neither of my parents was a great reader. My mother read popular magazines and an occasional novel; my father read technical books on carpentry and construction.

But this didn't stop you reading?

Well, my parents may not have read much themselves, but they encouraged me to read whatever I wanted and could find. The classic authors I remember reading first were Twain and Poe, like many other American youths, I don't doubt. A family of cousins in my mother's Georgia home town owned a complete set of Twain and I read through most of that while visiting one summer. We ourselves had a cheap edition of Poe and I dipped into that off and on, though he was never an author for me; probably he satisfied an adolescent whim for the gothic. We also owned, as I recall now, *Wuthering Heights* and something by Dumas; also *The Last of the Mohicans,* the only one of these I finished, although I did not like it much. I simply thought one ought to read famous books. These volumes came to us by way of a newspaper offer, each costing something like 39 cents. My taste had soon turned in favour of the books in the library – Dreiser and Dostoevski. *The Brothers Karamazov* was the great reading experience of those years. As far as I can judge, none of all this had anything at all to do with what I was later to write. I was reading poetry but not with the excitement and dedication with which I was reading fiction. In the summer before my last year of high school I did discover Eliot and his grandeur and exotic authority; Pound, too, with his smart-alec manner and cocksure odd opinions. The Untermeyer anthologies of those days were very instructive, and it was possible, I think, to distinguish easily enough between the serious poets and the fillers included. At least I felt that I could do so from the start.

I said just now that my parents encouraged me to read whatever I wanted to, but that was true only up to a point. There was a year in early adolescence when, hearing from me one too many 'radical' opinions, gleaned from reading, my mother forbade me to read any more Sinclair Lewis – of all people – for an entire year. This turned out to be as much of an aesthetic lesson, I have later felt, as a political or moral lesson.

Was it a happy childhood?

As I have only recently come to realize, it was a happy childhood, for which I have my parents to thank. My parents – and the then almost pastoral new city of Miami, which seemed to have every advantage but the cultural. And yet the public library was perfect for me at the time. I believe I must have read every book of poems in it over the years, without guidance, making my own small discoveries along the way. Sandburg and Kenneth Patchen are two I remember, and then, just a little later, Lowell and Elizabeth Bishop in new anthologies. When I was a freshman at the University of Miami, I was in the hospital for some while with a bad case of pneumonia: for reading I had ordered from New Directions, out of my saved-up allowance, Dylan Thomas's *The World I Breathe*, George Barker's *Selected Poems* and Jose Garcia Villa's new book, whose title I have forgotten. I was pleased with myself, I am sure, for having so unusual a reading list. My reading habits had begun to be formed that year of convalescence when I was ten, recovering from the osteomyelitis I have already mentioned. That year changed my life.

You've said it was a happy childhood, but it wasn't an untroubled one, was it? When you were eight years old, your paternal grandmother died; a year later, your best friend died after a long struggle with rheumatic fever; and not long after that, you became seriously ill with the osteomyelitis you've told us about, and had to miss a year of school. Any one of these experiences might have been expected to leave their mark on you. How about their combination?

I don't think I was sensitive or keen enough to have linked all that. Perhaps those things did connect in some pattern unknown to me. Of course they did over the years become the subjects of poems or at least the ground of experiences I would refer to in poems years afterwards.

You were drawn to music from an early age, starting the weekly sessions you've so lovingly described, both in poetry and in prose, when you were just five years old, and later on learning to play other instruments as well. Eventually, however, the desire to play was overtaken by the desire to compose, and the desire seems to have been a strong one, strong enough for you to conjecture that, if you'd had the right kind of encouragement and support at that time, you might now be writing music rather than poetry.

As for playing, I always enjoyed trying to read through new pieces more than practising for hours or weeks to perfect something. I would never have made a true pianist, lacking patience. My special skill or indulgence was sight-reading – moving on constantly to the new thing. My best friend and I shared that interest and that knack. We often played with four hands piano music intended for two hands, which meant that together we could produce a rough approximation of practically anything the first time through; oh, not without plenty of mistakes. Both of us decided at about the same time – when we were, say, fifteen – that we wanted to compose. My friend was probably more gifted musically than I was; he was later to support himself as a musician for many years. He was satisfied with the music of the past and was very fond of what we called 'the semi-classics'. I liked all that well enough myself but once I had heard *The Rite of Spring* on record, I was eager for more of the present, though anything contemporary was hard to come by in those days. Well, with the encouragement of the teacher-conductor, we both wrote concert pieces for our excellent high-school orchestra, and the orchestra performed both pieces on the same night, a heavy load for an audience, I am sure. I don't remember my friend's composition, but mine was terrible; no matter, I was pleased.

You've told us something about your reading at this time. I believe you were also trying your hand at writing?

At Christmas when I was fifteen, I received an inexpensive portable typewriter, more a toy than anything else. Whether I'd asked for it or not I can no longer say; in fact, I'd forgotten about it until this interview began to tap into my memory. It's altogether possible that my parents had had the bright idea of a typewriter on their own. In any case, on Christmas day itself, with fairly high and utterly unrealistic ambition, I sat down and began to type what I called my novel. Title: *A Boy of Fifteen*. Many adolescents must have done this kind of thing. Books never to be finished, of course; none of the novels I ever tried to write got farther than chapter one.

But now, pondering this question, I begin to recall that I had already been writing a little in the dead time between typing assignments in a secretarial class. What I wrote – and the form was just about the right length to be finished in those brief intervals – were cinquains, after the little five-line form invented by Adelaide Crapsey, and which I had come across somewhere. I remember liking the fact, even then, that very few people had heard of her. I don't remember writing any other poems that year, but it was a start of sorts. For my senior year in high school I transferred to a better school. There I met the first person of my age who was also interested in writing. This boy sat behind me in sociology class and one day he passed up to me a notebook with some sort of lyrical phrase written on each ruled line of the notebook. I whispered to him that I liked his poem. With a proper and rather impressive hauteur he observed that those lines were merely the first lines of some of his poems, and he would let me read the poems themselves if I liked. The poems were mostly sonnets, as he explained to me, and I began over the next few weeks to dash off a few sonnets myself. The first line of one of them for some reason sticks in my mind: 'It's all a big game, boys, come on, let's play'. This must have been around the time of Pearl Harbour, probably just before.

Did your literary inclinations get any encouragement?

I don't think I showed what I wrote to anyone at all during the first year or two. I encouraged myself, one might say. I had a falsely high regard for my own writing; and yet not altogether false, perhaps, considering the circumstances. The ambition I felt was always as high as my imagination would stretch. In college there was a little club for would-be writers – not very sophisticated but not altogether bland either – called the Snarks. In it I soon developed the reputation of being 'modernist' and 'obscure', a reputation I was careful to maintain. I was the group aesthete, I think; perhaps the whole school's aesthete. I had to do very little to qualify. There was not a lot of the little subterranean social clubbing together of the talented that used to go on and probably still does in British schools.

After graduating from high school in 1942, you went to the University of Miami, to study music. Why the University of Miami, I wonder? Would you not have liked to go somewhere further afield?

The University of Miami had a pretty good music school at the time, and one I was familiar with, but the main attraction was probably just that it allowed me to live cheaply at home. My parents bought me an old model A Ford to get back and forth to the university in. The music scholarship I had was for playing clarinet in the university band, which I enjoyed. Thoughts of going to school anywhere further afield did not, as far as I can recall, enter my head at the time. The university was adequate to all my social needs – I had any number of interesting friends – and would have been okay in music as well but for the fact that the male instructors were being drafted into the armed services, leaving the music faculty fairly well stripped. That was a blow. The teachers remaining, though nice enough, had to teach subjects they were not well prepared in, and it was all pretty dismal.

Pearl Harbour had been attacked in December 1941, and a good many of your contemporaries must have gone into the armed services. You, though, were declared unfit.

Yes, I escaped military service because of the osteomyelitis, for which I have always been tremendously grateful. I have a long scar still from the osteomyelitis and have had a couple of recurrences over the years, but that seems a very small price to pay, especially when I think of what Anthony Hecht and Louis Simpson, among American poets of my own generation, had to suffer. And of course there were the deaths of new friends – no sooner met than vanished.

It was while you were an undergraduate that you first encountered the composer Carl Ruggles. Did you know anything about him before you went to the university? Had you heard any of his music?

All I knew of Ruggles was what I had read in a newspaper article. I had heard none of his music; hardly anyone had. But I found an article in one of the serious music journals – *Modern Music* perhaps – comparing Ives and Ruggles. (Ives I knew nothing about either.) Reading that, I could at least imagine to some extent what this rare music might sound like.

I believe a recording of one or two of his works had been done, which at some point I managed to order from the obscure company that put it out. But that must have been later on. I did get some idea of Ruggles's work in the lesson periods, which were not done as a class but in private. It was his custom to spend much of the twenty or thirty minutes of a lesson demonstrating what he was currently working on – a dramatic demonstration, to be sure. The score – made up of pasted-together sheets of brown wrapping paper – would lie more or less flat atop the piano while he attempted to play simultaneously all the notes of a given chord with his stubby fingers, meanwhile singing out an important note here and there – but he did not have enough fingers to manage most of it. And I should not forget the cigar smouldering away at rest on the low keys as he played. Oh, it was all mysterious and enrapturing to me then.

According to Ruggles's biographer, Marilyn Ziffrin, he had been working as a part-time lecturer at the university since 1937, giving a twice-weekly seminar throughout the winter term. At its height, those seminars had attracted thirty or more students, but by the time you started to attend, the university's enrolment was well down, and Ruggles was no longer a part-time lecturer, but a consultant, addressing only a handful of advanced students. How were you, a freshman, able to attend those lessons of his, for which, presumably, you got no credits?

The regular composition teacher had been drafted; only Ruggles, an irregular sort of teacher, was left. There came a day when all those who thought they might want to study with Ruggles were summoned for auditions. Three of perhaps ten or twelve of us passed, and one of the three accepted soon dropped out. With the other survivor I still correspond; it interests me that he has spent his life as a painter. But in my most recent letter from him he mentions having just resumed work on an unfinished setting of 'When Lilacs Last in the Dooryard Bloom'd' that he had begun in school, back in the days when we were both studying with Ruggles. I too have taken up projects long abandoned, very nearly forgotten, but not yet quite lost. It is almost as if some of us lived in a great bubble of time in which the years went far more slowly than they did in reality, outside the bubble – and we and our ideas had about them still some of the freshness of youth. Not so, of course, merely an illusion, but a comforting one.

There did come a time when I thought of transferring to another school, prompted by Ruggles. I had written a woodwind quartet which he liked. He proposed that I go to Yale to study with Hindemith. I certainly couldn't afford that – I remember thinking, well, I would have to get a warm winter coat – but Ruggles was sure that on his word Hindemith would let me in to his class. I was not at all sure and, in any case, pondering the question for a couple of weeks, I realized that I was afraid of failure, of being exposed somehow, so I asked Ruggles not to pursue it. (Years later, at Yaddo, I happened to meet a composer who had been a member of Hindemith's master class at that time. He related an anecdote in which it happened that all of the students in the group had perfect pitch. I did not – and even all those years later I breathed a sigh of relief at such a confirmation that I had made the right decision.) Besides, my interest in writing *was* growing and deepening. (But I do still wish I could find a copy of the score of that woodwind quartet. I remember the first seven or eight bars of it; that's all.)

Ruggles is the second of four teachers to whose memory your 1987 collection, The Sunset Maker, *is dedicated. What was it about his teaching that you so admired?*

What I most admired hardly involved any details of the lessons themselves. What counted was the model he was in himself of the artist, the serious artist, one dedicated to the very highest ends.

What is your estimate of his music? Michael Tilson Thomas conducted a performance of Sun-Treader *at this summer's promenade concerts in London, but the notices I saw were lukewarm, written by critics most of whom seemed puzzled by Tilson Thomas's ongoing efforts to get Ruggles taken seriously.*

I'm not really qualified to pass judgement on Ruggles's music. I've listened to it all any number of times without coming to any defensible view of it. He has still a kind of cult reputation, I believe, at least in this country, and just that might have been enough to please him. I believe he always stood a bit apart, even in his own eyes. He is certainly an original. He loved sounds, especially, I think, sounds that no one had ever heard before, sounds most people would not have found beautiful but in which he could find beauty enough to exclaim over – and exclaim he would. 'Isn't that beautiful?!' – striking one of his strange, complicated chords. And the pupil would be obliged to say yes, for it *was* beautiful.

Ruggles is one of those gifted amateurs of the arts that America produced, especially in the early modern period – Marsden Hartley and Charles Burchfield among the painters, Charles Ives and Roy Harris among the composers, and Sherwood Anderson, perhaps Hart Crane, among the writers. For me these artists have long seemed the truly American type of artist, though not necessarily as profound or world-shaking as some of their contemporaries. Nevertheless they may be the ones we can be secretly most proud of.

At some point, you lost confidence in your talent for composition. What happened?

I realized I had a shaky sense of rhythm. Many of my friends in the band had a fine and intuitive sense of rhythm; mine was purely of the brain, not at all intuitive. A conscious effort had to be made. Also, I simply could not carry a tune, though I could write one down. It was embarrassing, a little; nor could I improvise. I could to some extent imagine what something would sound like when it was written down, but that wasn't good enough.

So after a few months, you gave up your musical studies ...

And moved over to literature, yes – which was a good deal less fun, and hardly more practical.

Whose writing would have been influential on you by this time?

Writers I was reading with some excitement included Hemingway, Yeats, Kenneth Patchen, Joyce (the first two books), James T. Farrell, Lawrence, anthologies of poetry, especially of the twentieth century. Mark Van Doren's bulky anthology of world poetry, printed on the thinnest paper I had ever come across.

When did it occur to you that you might have a vocation as a writer?

I think I can fairly say it never did take me that way. It just happened, and at some point it had grown to be too late to get out of it. If vocation was involved, I was, so to speak, converted and had taken my vows before I was aware of it. There must have come a point at which there seemed to be nothing else to do, but if I had to pinpoint the moment, it would probably have been the summer when I was considering the very remote possibility of Yale.

You met George Marion O'Donnell while you were at the University of Miami, and I believe he was he was very supportive.

O'Donnell was the first poet I met – a second-generation Fugitive-Agrarian from Vanderbilt, and a rival while there of Jarrell's, who was to publish his first and only collection in the New Directions *Five Young Poets* Series, along with Jarrell and Berryman. From Mississippi, he had also published the earliest, or one of the earliest, serious articles on Faulkner. A high-school friend of mine had the young O'Donnell as his freshman English instructor at Auburn and happened to show him some of the poems I had sent; perhaps my friend had asked me to send them, meaning to show them, as he did. Anyway, on the strength of perhaps half a dozen poems, O'Donnell invited me to visit him in Auburn, where he was teaching at Alabama Polytechnic Institute. I took the train up from Miami and there I was treated to talk about poems such as I had never heard before – Hardy, Blake, Dante, I remember – and in general treated like an adult.

That was in which year?

I was still a freshman.

And what did he think of your own poetry?

He corresponded with me regularly and generously about my poems, sharply critical at times, and very properly so. But the whole experience was heady and encouraging.

Do you recall any of the criticisms?

I do recall a question he put to me once. 'Why do you use no capitals to begin your lines?' My reply was something to the effect that I wanted to appear modem. 'But what about the Latin poets? They used no capitals either, and that was long ago.' After that – for the rest of my life, in fact – I have found it impossible to use lower-case letters to start off a line. I could do it, but it would have to be while smiling quietly to myself in memory of O'Donnell.

Did you stay in touch with him?

I don't know what happened to the friendship, but the correspondence gradually died, for no particular reason. To my great regret I was never to see him again. But for the strength of his influence I might have gone on and on trying to be 'experimental'.

Another poet you met while still an undergraduate was the somewhat better known Robert Frost.

Yes, in the early Forties Frost was wintering in South Miami. His daughter-in-law – Carol's widow – and his grandson Prescott, lived on the same property as the poet and did meals and other chores for him. Prescott was known as Bill to his friends at the University of Miami, which was conveniently near the Frost property. Bill enrolled there in the fall of 1943, I believe it was, and we became good friends. What seems remarkable to me now is that I had no particular interest in improving the opportunity to encourage Frost to talk about poetry; I don't remember asking a single question. Even at lunch, which I was invited to share once or twice with the Frosts, we scarcely spoke of poetry. I think it was because Frost knew – probably through Bill – that my favourite contemporary poet was Eliot, and this put me on the other side of the fence. He did not care for Eliot or Eliot fans, though in my presence he was never anything but polite about it. I thought of Frost as something of a sentimental poet and one who courted the middlebrow crowd, a hidebound traditionalist not at all in the vanguard, which is where I would have wished to be. I was not altogether wrong, I suppose. At a reading he gave at the university that winter or the next, he paused near the end and asked the audience for requests. I found this a little embarrassing, an entertainer's ploy that he should have been above, but I was even more embarrassed when the first member of the audience to respond with a request proved to be my composition teacher, fellow Vermonter Carl Ruggles. I wanted with all my adolescent heart the cold and austere high spirit (Joycean perhaps) of the artist to show, not that of the warm and folksy entertainer. I was not sophisticated enough to recognize Frost as the great poet of the age and his way of reading his work as the best there was. (After all, it was the first reading I had ever attended; they were rare in those days.)

You graduated from Miami in the spring of 1945, but it wasn't until the autumn of 1946 that you started to do postgraduate work at the University of North Carolina. What did you do in the intervening months?

Oh, I was really doing nothing. I got to New York City for the first time about then and was bowled over. I knocked about Greenwich Village for some months; I took a few odd jobs, and did some of the romantic things young would-be writers used to do – like hitchhiking and sleeping on subways.

Not, of course, doing any writing.

It wasn't a wrench, leaving Miami behind you?

Not at all. I was glad to flee, almost as glad as I would be now to be allowed to return to the Miami of that time. I simply did not realize how fine the place had been until it was no longer the place it had been. This is perhaps a common reaction to one's hometown looked back at after a certain amount of time.

The MA for which you enrolled at Chapel Hill, North Carolina, was in English. Apart from the classes in Chaucer – at one of which I believe you met your future wife, Jean Ross – do you remember what others you attended?

Renaissance, Shakespeare, early American, the transcendentalists, bibliography, etc.

In an interview you gave all the way back in 1966, you said that you didn't learn how to write poetry from your teachers, but from your friends and the books you were reading. I take it this wasn't a criticism of your teachers, since their subject was English, not Creative Writing?

I don't now remember what I intended to convey but I believe you put too polite an interpretation on it. Though sometimes interesting, the teaching was not notable. However, I did have some notable friends: the poets Edgar Bowers and Paul Ramsey, the novelist Richard Stem, and of course my wife Jean, who writes beautiful stories. And there were others who did not write but acted or did political things. Chapel Hill was headquarters of Southern left-wing politics in those days.

Did left-wing politics, or politics of any kind, hold any appeal for you?

I just assumed that everyone I knew was mildly left-wing. At Chapel Hill, among my acquaintances back then, you were as likely to meet a young Communist as a Republican. You didn't necessarily have to do anything to be accepted; just being on the right side seemed mostly good enough. Twenty years later it would have been different.

How did you and Edgar Bowers get to know each other? He was doing a BA rather than an MA, and in Modern Languages rather than English.

Edgar and I met through Paul Ramsey, a mutual friend, and fellow poet, who was, like us, a member of a little group of writers we put together – a club of sorts – that met, as well as I recall, every couple of weeks. During the meetings we read what we'd been writing and talked about it a little – friends together. Such clubs, such meetings, must have been occurring all over the world then, innocently enough, and might be thought of as a kind of predecessor of the later writers' workshops, now spread everywhere like an epidemic.

Bowers was very complimentary about you, saying that none of the poetry-writing friends he'd had at school or in the army 'was so knowledgeable as Don, with as much literary acumen, talent, and informed opinion or, I should really say, convictions.' How did he strike you?

The same, if you add in my Miami friend, Bob Vaughn.

I'll come back to him later, if I may. – Who were your poetic models while you were at Chapel Hill?

Yeats, Lowell (just then publishing *Land of Unlikeness*), Ransom, Tate, Hart Crane, a little of Delmore Schwartz, perhaps; others, doubtless, I no longer recall.

What about your prose models? I am right in thinking that your mind still wasn't made up at this time, as between becoming a poet and becoming a short story writer?

I thought I could do both. As it happens, I've managed to write and publish only five stories in all these years, the first two of which I no longer acknowledge. The writers of stories I especially liked were pretty obvious choices – Hemingway, Katherine Anne Porter, Eudora Welty (who had just published her first book), Joyce, early Faulkner. And I was much taken by Warren's *All the King's Men*, which was just out. It is one of the books I remember reading in a certain place – the porch of my Chapel Hill rooming house, perfect fall afternoons – and the very circumstances of the reading became part of the pleasure.

And the thesis you were working on? Can you tell us anything about that?

The subject of my MA thesis was the Fugitive-Agrarians. I tried to show how the ideas you found in their prose criticism turned up in their poems as well, especially their hatred of the abstract. Years later, I decided I wanted to read my old thesis and attempted to borrow it through interlibrary loan but was informed that the copy in the North Carolina library had been lost. Not getting to see it, though disappointing, probably saved me at least a little embarrassment.

You might not thank me for telling you this, but there is a copy in the Donald Justice Papers, stored in the University of Delaware Library.

How strange. I don't remember having a copy to send them. But how else would they have acquired it, if not from me?

Maybe they bought it from your alma mater? No, that can't be right, because I see now that what they have is only a carbon typescript, not a bound copy.

I think it must have come from me, in which case the subterranean truth could be that I didn't really want to read the thing again. Although my papers, such as they are, are in a perpetual state of chaos, and there must be things in my possession – a limited sort of possession, to be sure – of which I remain totally unaware. Still, this thesis business feels like a bit of a mystery to me.

Jean's sister, Eleanor, was married to Peter Taylor, who taught at the University's Woman's College, in Greensboro. Did you see much of them?

Chapel Hill and Greensboro were about fifty miles apart but somehow – I've forgotten how, maybe by bus – we did manage to visit briefly several times. A couple of times they drove over to Chapel Hill – once, I recall, with Cal Lowell, who was visiting them. The Taylors were very warm and generous to us – that summer we were their guests for a month in the country, in a fine old farmhouse near Norwood, North Carolina, where Jean and Eleanor had been born and brought up. The Taylors had bought the house there, which they called 'Scuppernong', after the regional grape, in part because the house had family associations, and in part simply because they liked old houses.

Randall Jarrell, an old friend of Taylor's, started teaching at Greensboro in the Fall of 1947. He'd just finished his stint as literary editor of the Nation, and was well on the way to becoming a power in the land. Did you have any contact with him at this time?

The first time I remember meeting Randall Jarrell was at the Arts Forum – as the springtime writers' conferences of the Woman's College were called – in the early spring of 1948. He made a big impression on everybody, I think – for his wit, his charm, his occasional acerbity. He was impassioned, assertive, and delicate all at once, bursting with enthusiasms. Hard to think now that he must have been barely thirty at the time. I still can't help thinking of him and Lowell and Peter as young gods in the literary world. I had read all or almost all of their published work – which wasn't yet very much in truth –

and this no doubt contributed to the mild form of awe I felt toward them. They accepted me as someone sitting at the edge of their circle and listening hard. I remember Jarrell making fun one afternoon of any poet who would lower himself by consulting the little rhyming dictionary in those days to be found at the back of the popular *Webster's Collegiate Dictionary*. (In those days we were more interested in rhyme than poets are today, of course.) I had been using that very rhyming dictionary myself quite recently and was somewhat embarrassed, but remember resolving with a sense of defiance to go on turning to the back of the book for help in rhymes whenever I needed to, which was pretty often. I was never very good at rhyming.

Another thing I remember about the Arts Forum is a game of croquet we played. The Forum was held in March and late snow lay in patches on the ground. In spite of that we got out the croquet set, put up a court in the Taylors' back yard, and played until the game fell apart with Lowell insisting on croqueting as many balls as he could as far as he could and Jarrell all the time trying to get him to concentrate on playing the game as it should be played.

Good practice for the croquet circle that De Snodgrass says you became a member of in Iowa, 'where tempers grew so fierce that several players did not speak for months at a time.'

My memory is softer – weeks of silence, maybe, not months. And to our credit, we did go on playing together the entire time.

The Greensboro student magazine, Coraddi, *had an Arts Forum issue, which included poems by you, Edgar Bowers and Paul Ramsey. Was that the first time you saw any of your own work in print?*

No, I'd had a poem in *Mademoiselle* as a freshman – early 1943, I think it was – not to mention poems and a short story or two in student magazines. It was O'Donnell who had arranged through his friendship with George Davis, one of the editors at *Mademoiselle*, to place a poem of mine there, in what was planned as a Southern issue. An odd coincidence: the other two poets included in the issue were Katherine Anne Porter (with a translation from the French) and Peter Taylor, whom I had not yet met.

I believe that some of your poems were discussed by Robert Penn Warren and Robert Lowell at the Arts Forum. Do you remember anything of what they said? Were they encouraging?

I don't happen to remember anything Lowell said; very likely he sa ˙ˈ⸜ ing or only polite little things about my poems. But I do vividly recalˡ describing the images in a couple of my poems as being like Rube Goldberg contraptions. Goldberg was famous at the time for his cartoons, which featured elaborate, zany, and pointless machines. Warren was quite right and my feelings were only very slightly bruised. I couldn't say that any of the criticism was encouraging, except perhaps in the sense that the poems were taken seriously; neither were the comments downright discouraging.

Incidentally, in attendance at that Arts Forum were a number of Kenyon College students, a carload or two of them. They had driven down from Ohio, a long way, and they were probably a good deal more formidable than our Chapel Hill contingent was. Anthony Hecht was among them, and his brother Roger.

I gather that poems by them were included in that same issue of Coraddi. *Do you remember what impression they made on you?*

We were very favourably impressed, of course, by Tony, but then he *was* a little older and more experienced than we were. There may have been a bit of the competitive spirit in the air − as when two athletic teams meet on neutral ground. It's possible that we were looked down upon as being from the culturally backward South (though the Kenyonites had as their teacher the classic Southerner himself, John Crowe Ransom). In any case, had there been some way of resolving the question, we would definitely have been the underdogs.

You obtained your MA in 1947, married Jean, and went back to the University of Miami, to do a year's stint as an English instructor. Was that the first time you'd done any teaching?

It was the first time I'd done any serious teaching. I had once put in four days teaching the seventh grade in a private school in Miami Beach just off the bay. It was the winter tourist season and we sat out under large beach umbrellas. Totally unprepared for the job, I passed some of the time reading the young pupils Hemingway stories, which they greatly enjoyed. At the end of the week, the principal discreetly asked me to show her my lesson plans for the coming week; having none, I decided I would do better as a bellhop, which turned out to be true enough.

Did you enjoy the university teaching?

Looking back, I can say that I enjoyed it, but it was hard work − four sections of freshman composition and one of world literature that first year. Many papers to mark. The students and I got along well together, which made it easier. There was time, some afternoons, after the last class, to hurry off to one of the thoroughbred race tracks or head off for the beach. This was, after all, Miami.

In the autumn of 1948, you went to Stanford, intending to do a PhD. Edgar Bowers was already there, doing an MA in English, and he had been encouraging you to go. The attraction was Yvor Winters, but I understand that you were only allowed to audit his classes, and received no credits for attending them.

It was the department chairman who, because of my teaching load as a graduate assistant, would only allow me to take one class each quarter, and in subjects like Old English or Restoration Drama. However, Winters himself was very willing to let me sit in on his classes, and I did so as often as I was in the mood and could spare the time.

You already knew In Defence of Reason?

Yes, it had come out only recently, but in good time to serve as the required text in the classes Winters taught. It had been a wedding gift from our friend Dick Stem.

Did its author live up to your expectations? By all accounts, he was a formidable figure.

Winters was an entirely formidable figure, to be sure. Authoritative, absolute in opinion – a mind already made up, with an obvious love for the literature he favoured, his own canon. Thinking back on it now, I would have to say that Winters did live up to my expectations, but I did not live up to his. He exceeded my expectations in one way at least: reading poems aloud. His voice would drop about a fifth in pitch, as if to indicate that he was now reading something deeply serious. He read slowly and expressively, strongly keeping the metre, his voice level, not particularly 'musical', as some might say, and certainly not dramatic. Recordings of Winters's readings that I've heard fall far short of the classroom readings, as, for instance, of Wordsworth's sonnet on Milton – not that he thought it one of the great poems of the language, but, as you heard him reading it, you were tempted to believe that it was. He was the best reader of poetry I ever heard, with the possible exception of Pound at his most theatrical – the polar opposite of Winters in reading style.

Is it possible for you to summarize what you learnt from Winters, what you went away from his classes knowing or understanding that you hadn't known or understood before?

Before I got to Stanford, though I was fascinated by the metres and indeed was attempting to use them, I did not have a very good hold on them. I think Winters's artful but clear and honest readings in class probably taught me more about the metres than anything else ever did. But aside from that – important as it was to me – I saw Winters mainly as a model – like Ruggles in this way – an exemplar of an artist's convictions coming to life in the work. I remember two things he said about the poems I was trying to write at that time. I had unawares slipped a hexameter into a passage of blank verse; Winters spotted it and let it be known that he considered it an error, inadmissible. And in another poem he objected to a pun I had tried on the word 'rest'. When I mentioned in my defence that George Herbert had used the same pun, he remarked that in the Herbert poem the pun was well done, in mine not. Which was probably true. I remember too – and some might find it interesting – that the first (and I think only) assignment in his poetry writing class was this: to write a description of a natural scene in heroic couplets in the style of Crabbe. Needless to say, the class size was immediately reduced, which had probably been at least half the reason for the assignment.

But you left Stanford after only one year. Was that because you were finding it difficult to make ends to meet? I understand that you and your wife were both having to work.

We had a rough time of it financially, all right, but most of our friends did also. No, I left because I saw myself as being permanently in chains as a graduate assistant, making no useful progress whatever toward the degree.

Did you feel bitter about this turn of events?

I don't remember feeling bitter about any of it, though I was disappointed that Winters had not cared for what I wrote. On the whole, the year had been pretty exciting.

And you did win a prize in the annual Creative Writing Contest, for 'The Doctor's Wife', a short story.

The second prize, yes, which was worth $150. That gave us enough money for the train fare back to Miami.

Where you resumed work as a university instructor. Did you see this as a temporary expedient? If so, what were your longer-term plans?

I don't remember thinking of my job at the University of Miami as a temporary expedient. I still wanted to write. I think I must vaguely have figured I would go on meeting freshman composition classes till I was old and grey, by which time I would have become a good poet, with plenty of money from the novels I would have been writing. Something like that. The only other prospect I remember considering, and that not very seriously, was gambling in the afternoons at the great racetracks of Miami and in the evenings at the greyhounds.

In 1951, you published a pamphlet, The Old Bachelor and Other Poems. *This was a small press publication, with just ten numbered pages. What went into it?*

Early poems went into it, including several I had written at Stanford with some hope of pleasing Winters. The title poem – a dramatic monologue mostly in iambic pentameters rhyming without much of a pattern and featuring, as printed up, a couple of typos – suffered under the illusion that there was something that could be identified and even praised as Southern writing, and that it mattered. A sonnet pair wasn't bad, and I think the magazine or two to which I had vainly submitted them made a mistake not publishing them. The prejudice against verse in metres and with rhyme had not yet, in those long-ago days, settled in, but perhaps was beginning.

How did the pamphlet do?

I think it may possibly have sold out, all to a local audience. I doubt that any copies escaped from Florida, even from Miami's Dade County.

The year after The Old Bachelor, *and three years after leaving Stanford, you entered the University of Iowa's Writers' Workshop, to work for the PhD they were offering in Creative Writing. How did that come about?*

There came a year when in the late spring virtually all of us young instructors were 'let go' by the University of Miami, probably in order to troll for newcomers, who could be had somewhat more cheaply. The pleasant dream of a lazy Miami existence was blasted. Peter and Eleanor Taylor allowed us to live in their grand old house in the small town of Hillsborough, North Carolina, while they stayed in Greensboro. There we led a wonderfully charmed life for several months, with our inadequate savings leaking away all too rapidly. The hope was that I might sell a story for good money, and I did come fairly close. Still, when Peter and his friend Robie Macauley, seeing that I was getting nowhere fast, suggested that I write to Paul Engle at the University of Iowa, I acted quickly, with some sense of desperation. Paul was running one of the then two writing programs in the country, the other being Stanford. (Now there must be hundreds, for better or worse; probably worse.) Robie himself had recently graduated from Iowa, and I believe both he and Peter dashed off letters to Iowa recommending me. It worked, and Paul wrote back immediately offering me an assistantship to teach fiction writing. (I had published my first short story and had it anthologized.) Jean and I moved in with my parents in Miami, saving money until the mid-year school term was to start, and I found a job driving a cab – a job I'd always had a hankering for. It turned out to be a terrible job, and I was unable to earn enough at it to save any useful amount of money. We sold our car to pay our bus fare up to Iowa. (We had done the same a few years before to get bus fare to Stanford.)

Your fellow students at Iowa included William Belvin, Jane Cooper, Henri Coulette, Robert Dana, William Dickey, Philip Levine, Don Petersen, William Stafford, W.D. Snodgrass and your friend from Chapel Hill, Richard Stern. It must have been an exciting place to be?

I think all of us were excited, except possibly Bill Stafford, who was older – and calmer. The excitement wasn't limited to the classes, although the weekly workshop sessions were good enough to look forward to. The life of the town was exciting in itself. We used to say it was the only place in America where you could tell people you were a poet and be respected for it. An exaggeration, I don't doubt, but we did say it. I mean, we would have been exaggerating to speak of anything like unconditional respect – but there really was a slim chance of it, it seemed.

Amongst the teachers you had at Iowa were John Berryman, Robert Lowell and Karl Shapiro, with each of whom you spent a term. I believe you thought Berryman the best teacher?

I did think he was the best, yes, and a large part of how good he was had to do with his very character, however much a few have maligned him. He was full of a kind of fervour or fire, in class and out. In class he was a master of detail and care; he was in love with the whole business of reading and writing and of talking about it, in love with teaching itself, though he had not done much of it. I wouldn't call him a model exactly, not an example, as with others. His chief difference from the other teachers I had was that he was truly interested in what you were doing. Berryman, Lowell and Shapiro were all terribly self-involved – as what poet is not? – but Berryman had room in his capacious heart to become involved in what you were doing as well – and to care about it.

You seem to have made as much of an impression on him as he did on you. Dana, Snodgrass and others have all written about his excited reaction to your work. Snodgrass recalls a day on which all of you had handed in your assignments. Berryman 'sat at his desk idly leafing through them, then stopped, stared, and read one of the sonnets to himself. His face aghast, he then turned to the class and said, "It is simply not right that a person should get a poem like that as a classroom assignment!"' The poem in question was 'The Wall', and another of the students who met him for a beer later that week – unnamed, but quoted by Berryman's biographer, John Haffenden – recalls how Berryman 'immediately began to read [the sonnet] and ... marvelled at [its] opening and the explosive pause in the second line. He was deliriously excited and to this day I can hear him recite it: "The wall surrounding them they never saw; / The angels often."' Did Berryman's reaction to your poem strike you as forcefully as it struck your fellow students?

Everyone seems to have his own version of that story. My version, which I think is the true one, is less dramatic. It's just that Berryman had phoned me the night before the class meeting to tell me how much he liked the poem. Such enthusiasm was unexpected, such kindness. What happened in class the next day I really can't recall, except for a faint memory of comments he made regarding some sound effects in that sonnet which I had not been aware of and in fact doubted the effect of, though I'm sure I refrained from saying anything to soften the praise I was getting.

This wasn't an easy time in Berryman's life, was it? His wife had left him the previous summer, he'd been out of work and drinking a great deal. The night he'd arrived in Iowa, he'd fallen down the stairs of his boarding house, crashed through a glass door, broken a wrist and sustained some heavy bruising. Were his emotional problems as obvious to his students as his physical problems must have been?

Maybe to others the problems were obvious. Not to me. At least not then. I thought he was living constantly at some kind of emotional peak, like someone on speed, perhaps. But it was, after all, an exciting time for most of us and there were a lot of supercharged guys around. In any case, I tend to remain blind to such matters, and accepting of them.

But Haffenden and Mariani both recount the early morning phone-call Berryman made, begging you to go over to his apartment because he was thinking of killing himself. 'I got a cab and went right over,' Haffenden reports you as saying. ' When I looked from the hall through his living room door, I saw him sitting on the floor (in bathrobe, I believe) regarding an open case of old-fashioned razors. The sight was too much for me. I felt faint and had to lie down on the sofa. He became immediately all concern and consideration, hurrying down to the bathroom to fetch damp cloths with which to chafe my wrists and so on. Soon I was feeling more myself. To my great relief, so was he.'

Well, of course that incident made me realize how desperate he often was. But John had a capacity for joy as well as suffering, and that's something discussions of him often ignore. There were calm afternoons drinking beers together in some of the great little taverns of Iowa City. I remember a remark of his from one such afternoon: 'Thank God I never fell under the influence of Yeats myself.' At first I thought he must be joking.

And he wasn't? How very odd. Because he did acknowledge the influence quite freely later on in his life, didn't he?

I've always told the story with Berryman referring to Yeats, but now, with your prompting, it occurs to me that, considering how much worse my memory seems to be getting, it might have been Auden, not Yeats. Berryman's comment, in either case, still seems pretty startling to me. Perhaps we were in that tavern for longer than I remembered.

What did you make of Lowell's teaching? Snodgrass thought he was marvellous: 'However high our expectations,' he said, 'no one was disappointed by Lowell's teaching.' But Philip Levine, for one, was disappointed. He told Paul Mariani that Lowell played favourites with the students, badly misread a great deal of the poetry under discussion, was fiercely competitive, and wasn't above overwhelming the class with one of his own poems. 'In fairness,' Levine added, 'he was teetering on the brink of a massive nervous breakdown ... Rumours of his hospitalization drifted back to Iowa City, and many of us felt guilty for damning him as a total loss.' Who was closer to the truth, would you say – those who thought him marvellous or those who thought him a total loss?

I thought Lowell was an excellent teacher. He was someone of great intensity, to whom everything mattered. There was a distance, a decent and probably self-protective distance, but I approve of that, if approval matters. As well, I liked him a lot personally, and he was always very kind to me. All the same, if I don't remember him quite the way Phil does, it's nevertheless true that Lowell was more interested in what he himself was writing than in what his students were doing. I remember him reading to us one afternoon an early version of his longish Marie de Medici poem – early in that it was still in his familiar rhyming pentameters – and ending by inviting comments from the class. Of course we thought it was pretty wonderful, but the chorus of praise wasn't quite unanimous, and Lowell was dismayed. It's also true that there was a hint of condescension in his regard for student work. This was almost certainly well deserved, of course, but still ...

So Berryman was the more endearing teacher?

Berryman went further with us, and we who admired him could not help liking him for a kind of selflessness. But to go back to your original question, my guess is that between those who thought Lowell marvellous and those who thought him a loss – certainly not a *total* one – we would have had at least a small majority on the marvellous side.

What about Shapiro?

Shapiro was less interesting, but some of us were very fond of his new Adam and Eve sequence of poems, which had recently come out in *Poetry*. Some admirer had clipped out the pages containing the sequence from the library copy, a dirty trick, frustrating the rest of us, at least for a time. As a matter of fact, I suspect that that sequence had something to do with the sonnet we talked about a few moments ago ...

'The Wall'?

Yes.

I've had a look at that sequence, and the connection isn't hard to find. It's there in the very first poem, 'The Sickness of Adam', which also features an angel unfurling its wings

> For it said nothing but marvellously unfurled
> Its wings and arched them shimmering overhead,
> Which must have been the signal from the world
> That the first season of our life was dead.

I'm no angelologist, but my guess is that your angel belonged to a considerably higher order than Shapiro's.

But of Shapiro's classes I remember only one remark – to the effect that we should never use anything literary as subject matter. (Surely my memory strays here; no one as good as Shapiro could possibly dogmatize quite so unreasonably.) I had just shown him a sonnet I had done on Hamlet's father – or else I went home from class and wrote one – I've forgotten which now. At least his criticism, if that's what it was, had some effect.

De Snodgrass remembers the first few lines of that sonnet –

As Hamlet the king was sleeping in his garden
His brother poured some poison in his ear.
He felt, at once, his limbs begin to harden
And the red leaves were tangled in his hair.
And, suddenly, he turned so pale no one
Could see him.

– and he's written about them, admiringly, enviously: 'It seemed – it still seems – the best joke in any poem I know. But even if I hadn't been able to cap those lines, to finish a sonnet which maintained at least that level, even if I hadn't been able to add so much as one line to what is there, I'd have invented a new form for it, have titled it "Fragment", have found some way to put those lines in print.'

I can't help being cheered up by De's remarks – practically the nicest thing anybody has ever said about my work. Too bad it's about a poem I tossed out years ago, thinking it not quite up to snuff. I wish I had it back now. All I can do is polish up the lines as De – amazingly – remembers them. Thanks to De I have been able to reconstruct the first stanza of the sonnet and another phrase or two. Here is the correct version of the beginning, if anybody cares – an example of the persistence of memory:

One summer while the king slept in his garden
His brother poured a poison in his ear.
Before he woke, his limbs began to harden,
And there were red leaves tangled in his hair.

.... he had grown so pale
No one could see him; no one heard him shout.

At this point the poem abruptly blanks out for me; I cannot go on. Perhaps one day it will come back to De.

Politically, this was a troubled time. The Rosenbergs had been executed in 1953, causing great controversy; Senator McCarthy was at the height of his powers; and right across the country schoolchildren were being made to participate in air raid drills, the purpose of which was to prepare them for the possibility of nuclear attack. How much of this turmoil affected you and your peers at Iowa?

De Snodgrass was obviously affected, though if he had started *Heart's Needle* by then, it remained a secret. And Don Petersen in *The Spectral Boy*, his only book, calls up the very hot summer when we gathered around his TV –

TVs were rare among our crowd – watching with great partisanship and a certain amount of nervous apprehension the McCarthy hearings. But we talked politics much less than we talked poetry. A little more than a decade later – the Vietnam War – that was different.

You are quite a gambler, by the sounds of it: horses, dogs, jai alai, poker ... Where did this interest in gambling come from?

I always liked games. Growing up in Miami, I got interested in thoroughbred racing and, through the greyhound schooling races, to which kids were admitted, in the dogs too. I still think a happy retirement could be spent within walking distance of a thoroughbred track. Sunny afternoons, the Daily Racing Form, a few bucks to risk – what could be finer? Unfortunately, I live a great many miles from the nearest track. Jai-alai my friends always liked better than I did, I don't know why. And poker – well, I still enjoy that. I don't want to give the impression that any of this was big-time; I always played within the limits of what I could afford to lose. Well, almost always.

But the poker you played with Nelson Algren the year he was in residence at Iowa was supposed to have been for high stakes.

Fairly high, for the time. Nothing like what the pros go for. Nelson loved to play and didn't mind losing – probably lost the equivalent of his salary for his year of teaching, a job he appeared to despise except that it supported his poker luck, which was bad.

You obtained your PhD, and were given a Rockefeller fellowship, with which, in late 1954, you travelled to Europe. Was the trip a significant one for you?

The fellowship came, I have always believed, as the result of a letter Berryman wrote for me. He gave me a copy, which I kept for years, may still have somewhere. My wife and I planned to stay the year in Europe, but our fellowship money, which was not in fact very much, ran out after three or four months. Postwar Europe was not nearly as inexpensive as we had foolishly been led to believe. Anyhow, the whole trip began with an omen of disaster. Our first ship rammed into a Norwegian freighter off Nantucket Lightship – in almost the same spot the Andrea Doria sank not long after. Very thrilling but also very scary. (One of the other passengers on our ship happened to be John Cage, but it would be more than twenty years before we met.) In some ways the collision was the high point of our trip. We met no one, did nothing of any consequence, and enjoyed ourselves as long as the money held out. In the end we had to cable my father for return fare, which was mildly humiliating at the age of twenty-nine.

41

Back in the States, you taught for a while at the University of Missouri at Columbia and for a time at Hamline University, St Paul, Minnesota. Then, in 1957, you were asked to go back to the Writers' Workshop in Iowa, to take over while the director, Paul Engle, was away on leave. This was to have been a short-term thing, but you ended up staying for the better part of a decade. You must have found the place and the work very congenial.

Yes, indeed. So much so that, whenever I left – which I did several times over the years, and always, it seemed to me, for good reason – there would eventually come a time when we decided we liked no place better and we would return. When I retired from the University of Florida, we returned for what I suppose must be the last time. Having run into an especially hard winter this year, though, I must admit we are thinking of Florida again.

In 1960, Wesleyan University Press brought out your first full collection, The Summer Anniversaries. How did that come about? It was only the second year Wesleyan had been publishing poetry. Were you approached by them or they by you?

It's a fairly complicated little story and very likely boring to anyone not involved. Here's what happened. Jerome Rothenberg had started a small press, The Hawk's Well, and meant to publish my book. I've forgotten who put the two of us in touch. Jerry had just published the American edition of Thom Gunn's *Fighting Terms*, which was certainly a favourable sign. But I think there was a problem getting it or some other Hawk's Well Press book through customs from somewhere in Europe, where it had been printed. This caused a lengthy delay, which meant there wasn't yet enough money on hand to publish my book on the expected schedule. In the meantime the Wesleyan University Press was just beginning to publish books of young poets – Louis Simpson and James Wright among them – a great start. The director of the press approached me about a manuscript. But I owe its publication to the kindness of Don Hall. He was on some sort of board there, I believe, which chose the books to be published, and he, I am told, recommended my book to the press. (I did not know Don at the time, but we had something in common, both of us having studied at Stanford with Winters.) And Jerry Rothenberg seemed glad of my chance to go with a bigger press than his own Hawk's Well and was perfectly willing to release me from our agreement.

In 1955 you'd written a poem which one might have expected to see included in the book, since it bore the same title, 'The Summer Anniversaries'. Instead, the book included an extensively revised version of that earlier poem, which you entitled 'Anniversaries'. Only a couple of lines from the three-

stanza original survived into its four-stanza successor, but this was only the beginning of the story. When your Selected Poems *came out, in 1979, the original poem was included amongst the uncollected pieces that were printed at the back of the book, and its successor had disappeared. Then, when your* New and Selected Poems *came out, in 1995, we were given yet another version – one which revived the original's second stanza while dropping its successor's second. You'd also gone back to calling it 'The Summer Anniversaries'.*

All of the versions of that poem, no matter what the title, I look on as the same poem, the same poem seeking – and unfortunately never finding – its ideal form and expression.

What was getting between you and the poem's ideal form and expression – its 'platonic script', as you've called this notional thing elsewhere? Can you say?

One of the reasons, I suspect, that I remained permanently disappointed in this poem, in all its guises, is that it's written in the three-stress line Yeats and Auden used so beautifully, and it began to seem to me that they had used it up, as if nobody would ever be entitled to use it again.

Richard Stern recalls an unpublished stanza of the poem, included in a letter you sent him before the first version appeared in print.

> A pleasant red-haired man
> Noticing my red hair
> Predicted a great career,
> But for the asking mine,
> Though whether of sword or pen,
> Confessed he could not tell,
> So cloudy was the ball.
> Now how could a person
> Know that words from a stranger's mouth
> Could seem the simple truth
> To a boy of seven or eight?

Yes, but Dick's memory fails him in lines eight and nine, whose metre he wrongs.

Well, the metre could be restored quite easily, by breaking those lines after 'know' rather than 'person', and maybe dropping 'Now', but that would still leave us with an eleven- rather than a twelve-lined stanza, and the rhyme scheme – which is pretty irregular, but doesn't allow for unmated lines – would be unsatisfied. But perhaps this was written before you'd settled on the stanza length and rhyme scheme the published versions employ?

No, I don't think so. We clearly need a line to slant-rhyme with 'eight', but for the life of me I can't remember what it was.

David Galler, in a hostile, even aggressive, review of The Summer Anniversaries, *wrote you off as an epigone of Ransom, Empson and Stevens. But Galler aside, nobody else seems to have detected the influence of Stevens on your first book, and this surprises me, since 'Ladies by Their Windows', which is a very fine poem, I take to be unthinkable save as the work of someone who'd looked long and hard at Stevens's work.*

Galler's was by no means the only hostile review, though I've been told he changed his mind later. One thing that is rarely made clear to me in reviews is why the reviewer dislikes what he is objecting to, or, if he's commending something, why it is he likes it. Oh, once in a while it's made clear ...

Yes, but one's used to the 'chorus of indolent reviewers' settling for a huff or a puff.

Anyway, you are certainly right about the debt to Stevens in 'Ladies by Their Windows', but I make no apology for that; what I think of as the tradition lives and is carried on in part by such dependencies and allegiances. Though I consider 'Ladies by Their Windows' too heavily in debt myself.

How big an influence on The Summer Anniversaries *was Weldon Kees? If you hadn't happened on* The Fall of the Magicians, *you obviously wouldn't have written your 'Sestina on Six Words by Weldon Kees' – whose point of departure was that book's 'Sestina: Travel Notes' – but would you agree that the influence went deeper than that?*

By the time I discovered Kees for myself, early in 1955, about half the poems in my first book had already been written. Doubtless there was some influence, but I think it comes down mostly to my trying to use a very flat style without losing all sense of the poetical – or even to trying to make the flat style itself fully poetical, and in a way different from such a free-verse master as Williams.

It's the stripped-down or unadorned nature of much of the writing in this volume that makes me inquire about the influence of Kees – that and the darkish subject-matter.

Yes, a sense of despair hung over Kees's work like smoke, and that probably had some influence too.

There's a fair amount of autobiographical material in your first collection. If we go back to 'Anniversaries', for example, we find that its speaker and you have quite a lot in common. Both of you were born under the sign of Leo; both of you were hospitalized at the age of ten and underwent surgery which left you with a scar; both of you remember a time in your late teens when you spent time practising at the piano while other boys kicked a ball around outside ... I'm told that Japan wasn't rocked by an earthquake on the day you were born, as it was on the day the poem's speaker was, but Honshu was hit by a severe quake a little earlier in the year, and maybe you were thinking of that ...

I think the earthquake I was referring to took place in 1923, not 1925, but this was a long time ago. I was trying to get a certain tone via dramatic exaggeration.

Well, my point is that you have never shunned the autobiographical, though you are known to be hostile to certain ways of accommodating it. Can I ask you to say something about this?

You're right that there's a fair amount of autobiographical material in this poem – and not only this poem. It's just that I don't wish to parade it as such; I want to treat the personal stuff as impersonally as if I were making it all up.

But that makes it sound like a personal preference, where I take it that you regard this as a matter of aesthetic principle?

I do.

The Summer Anniversaries was winner of the Lamont Award for 1959. How important a development was that?

Fairly important, I would say, in a small way. Prizes help to get your work taken seriously; that may have been truer in 1960 than it is today – there are so many prizes now compared to then.

The book received a number of positive reviews, and a number of negative ones too. Did any of the reviews, positive or negative, influence you in any way?

I don't think the reviews influenced me at all, though the negative ones did make me angry.

Do you remember what you made of the review Witter Bynner wrote for Poetry, which had it that there were two Donald Justices, one of them 'a telling new person, alive with poetry,' the other 'a totally different person ... with no telling voice,' and which went through the book saying who was responsible for what?

I recall being grateful for it, no matter how odd it seemed. Bynner had no axe to grind.

But could you make any sense of the way he divided things up? It left me baffled, I must say. And while I can understand your having been grateful, it's a perfect example of the sort of review we decried a little earlier, huffing here, puffing there, and not bothering to offer any kind of explanation.

I've just looked it up again after many years and can report that I would have divided up the good and bad differently myself, quite differently.

One of the folders Robert Dana kept from his days as a student at Iowa contains four of your poems. Handwritten in the margins of one of them are the lines of Yeats's 'A Deep-Sworn Vow':

> Others because you did not keep
> That deep-sworn vow have been friends of mine;
> Yet always when I look death in the face,
> When I clamber to the heights of sleep,
> Or when I grow excited with wine,
> Suddenly I meet your face.

Alongside these lines is a note recording Berryman's classroom judgement: 'One of the greatest poems in English, I think.' Unfortunately, Dana doesn't say which of your poems appears on the page containing these items, but I wonder, could it have been 'Love's Map', later retitled 'A Map of Love'?

> Your face more than others' faces
> Maps the half-remembered places
> I have come to while I slept –
> Continents a dream had kept
> Secret from all waking folk
> Till to your face I awoke,
> And remembered then the shore,
> And the dark interior.

There are big differences between the poems, of course – to pick on only one, yours is a love poem, where Yeats's is better described as an encomium – but the resemblances strike me as more than merely accidental, and it wouldn't surprise me if they'd struck Berryman that way too.

The Berryman class was in 1954, and my poem wasn't written until 1958 or 1959.

Ah.

What I think you've turned up is a sort of echo – not a very loud one, I hope – of a Yeats poem I had known for some time (as I recall, it was used in *Understanding Poetry*, a book that had some influence on my thinking, as it did on that of many young writers at the time).

'Love's Map' was one of the poems that Bynner would have thrown out, inexplicably from my point of view.

Bynner was not the only one. Dudley Fitts in the *New York Times Book Review* went out of his way to find 'map' a pun of unbearable grossness; he professed to believe that I was unacquainted with the slang meaning of 'map'.

Another of the poems Bynner would have thrown out, just as mysteriously, was your 'Sestina on Six Words by Weldon Kees', which I mentioned a little earlier. Is it true that you'd sent Kees a copy of the poem just before his disappearance – his car was found abandoned on the northern approach to the Golden Gate Bridge in July 1955, and the suspicion was that he'd either killed himself by jumping into the bay or else had gone off to start a new life in Mexico – and that the envelope had come back to you marked 'Return to Sender'?

I don't know where that story came from. In fact, I was still trying to find an address for him when I heard about his disappearance.

You might want to have a word with Jim Reidel, who kindly sent me some of the chapters from his forthcoming biography of Kees. It was from one of those that I heard the story about your poem's being returned.

Well, I can assure you that's wrong. I learned of Kees's disappearance from Ray B. West, editor of the *Western Review*, whose house in Iowa City we were renting that summer. Ray had just returned from San Francisco, and I'm pretty sure I asked him if he knew how I could get in touch with Kees, only then to have him tell me the West Coast news, that Kees had disappeared.

In that case, there's something else you need to speak to Reidel about, because he thinks you learned about the disappearance from an obituary notice in Poetry.

Even if I had had an address, I might not have written Kees, always having been reluctant to force myself on people I don't know.

Well, these are minor matters, to be sure, but worth getting straight, since it's in the gaps between such facts as can be established that the myths so readily take root. – What was your reaction to the news of Kees's disappearance?

Great disappointment. Not that it would have made any difference, really, but I wished the poem had been finished in time for him to have seen that there was at least one very devoted fan somewhere in the world. He felt like a neglected poet and was in truth neglected.

You say you were disappointed, but you must surely have been shocked too ...

Certainly ...

I mean, someone reading the poem in ignorance of when it was written could easily be forgiven for thinking, not just that it had been written after Kees's disappearance, but with that disappearance in mind.

> I often wonder about the others
> Where they are bound for on the voyage,
> What is the reason for their silence,
> Was there some reason to go away?
> It may be they carry a dark burden,
> Expect some harm, or have done harm.

Yes, I see how the poem could seem to have come after the disappearance, even to refer to the disappearance itself, in a general way. But it just wasn't in fact prophetic; I did not see the future.

When your sestina was published in The Hudson Review *a couple of years later, I understand that Kees's father saw it, and that he wrote to you, hoping that the six teleutons – 'others', 'voyage', 'silence', 'away', 'burden', 'harmed' – might supply a clue to his son's disappearance. They didn't, of course, but you and he exchanged letters, and at some stage it was agreed that you would edit a selection of his son's poems. Was this your idea or his? And what exactly did the two of you have in mind?*

The idea for a book of Kees's work was mine, but it was prompted by the desire of a friend, Kim Merker, whose Stone Wall Press was to do many beautiful hand-press books over the years to come. He wanted to do a substantial printing job on his hand-press and asked me to suggest a poet whose work he and his partner, Raeburn Miller, could undertake to print. I proposed doing a Selected Kees, figuring he would appear a stronger poet if what I took to be the unevenness of his poems was made less apparent in a Selected version than in a Collected version it would be. But Harry Duncan, a master printer and the teacher of Merker and Miller, persuaded us to do the long version, a monster job for inexperienced young printers to start off with. Yet they brought it off handsomely, as anyone who has seen the rare Stone Wall Press edition would agree, I feel sure. John Kees, the poet's father, would naturally enough have preferred a larger edition than Merker and Miller could produce by hand, for it was the father's hope that someone might see the book who could somehow help to find his missing son. He was disappointed that there would be no photograph of his son in the book, which might, as he reasoned, have aided recognition. But he was unfailingly co-operative and grateful. Later it was he who arranged for the University of Nebraska Press – the Kees family was from Nebraska – to do the paperback version. I had no hand in that; in fact, it came as a surprise to me, very welcome, of course.

In your recent collection of essays, Oblivion, *you tell of a friend of Kees's who claimed to have encountered him in a bar in South Pasadena several years after his disappearance. Jim Reidel tells me that there have been a handful of such sightings, the earliest of them going back to 1957, when another friend of the poet's claimed to have encountered him in the bookstore of a Texas University.*

Reidel's anecdote of the sighting in Texas is one I haven't heard, but there've been others – in Provincetown, in Manhattan ...

I believe the San Francisco Examiner *even had a front-page story in the late Eighties by Pete Hamill, a well-known journalist who claimed to have met Kees a couple of years after his disappearance, once again in Mexico, once again in a bar. Hamill hasn't responded to Reidel's requests for further information, and Reidel doesn't take this story any more seriously than the others, despite its author's status. As far as he's concerned, all the stories are born out of wish-fulfilment: 'People did not want to let him go.' Is that your opinion too?*

It is. Many missing persons must over the years have been sighted, especially in bars. It's all a part of the mythic context.

Between 1964 and 1965, you were on leave of absence from Iowa – where you'd been promoted to Associate Professor – going to the Actor's Workshop in San Francisco as a Ford Foundation Fellow in Theatre. What did you do during this period?

What I did was to attend rehearsals and performances of the theatre company – which was a very good one – and to try to write plays. The general idea behind the Ford Foundation program was that writers might actually learn something about theatre and thus something about how to write stageworthy plays, from being allowed to sit in on a theatre's productions. I went on writing poems and did try to write short plays. (One later became the libretto for a one-act opera composed by a friend of mine, Edward Miller.) John Hawkes was also attached to the Actors' Workshop that year. He managed to write a number of plays, better received by the theatre people than my feebler efforts, thus exciting my envy. But the company was offered a chance to move to New York and become the resident company at Lincoln Centre – and how could they refuse such an offer? – though as it turned out their first season in New York was to prove a disaster. Anyhow, the San Francisco company broke up, leaving its two writers-in-residence rather happily stranded. Over all this hovered the cloud of the Vietnam War, which was just getting revved up. I know I became depressed and was glad to flee the west coast for the sanctuary of Miami. Incidentally, while out there I met Michael Grieg, who had been Kees's best friend, though I made no attempt to pick over the bones of Kees's San Francisco years. Why that was I can't really say. Years later Grieg and I were to become rather good friends.

Didn't he publish a villanelle about Kees in the same year you published your sestina about him? Since when, of course, there've been any number of poetic tributes.

I've forgotten the villanelle. At one time I began collecting poems about Kees – all of them, as well as I recall at the moment, involved his disappearance. But I gave up on the project. It became too big. And then some of the poems were naturally a lot better than the others.

Your second collection, Night Light, *came out in 1967. It's a very different book from* The Summer Anniversaries, *and must have surprised those of your admirers who'd not kept track of the small press publications you'd brought out in the intervening years –* A Local Storm *in 1963 and* Sixteen Poems *in 1966. The book contains a poem which some have taken to be straightforwardly critical of the sort of thing you'd included in* The Summer Anniversaries. *I'm talking about 'Early Poems', of course, which reads as follows:*

How fashionably sad my early poems are.
On their clipped lawns and hedges the snows fall.
Rains beat against the tarpaulins of their porches,
Where, Sunday mornings, the bored children sprawl,
Reading the comics before the parents rise.
– The rhymes, the metres, how they paralyze.

Who walks out through their streets tonight? No-one.
You know these small towns, how all traffic stops
At ten; the corner streetlamps gathering moths;
And the pale mannequins waiting in dark shops,
Undressed, and ready for the dreams of men.
– Now the long silence. Now the beginning again.

What most of the people who've seized on this poem have failed to notice is that it exemplifies precisely those qualities it appears to disparage. In other words, its dominant mood is one of sadness, and its lines are both rhyming and metrical.

You're quite right, of course, and how any reader could have missed the point, which seems if anything all too obvious, has always puzzled me. But I think you are the first person who's ever got it right in public. If readers can't get this simple business right, how can they read the language's really difficult poets?

Night Light is something of a mixed bag, formally. Metrical and rhyming poems like the one just discussed consort with poems written in syllabics, poems written in free verse, poems written in prose. Bruce Bawer has called the book an 'experimental' work, which would be unexceptionable were it not for the suggestion, rendered explicit in the course of his essay, that the book represents a kind of recul pour mieux sauter. I take it that this is a view you would resist?

Yes, I would. One might suppose all this could prove interesting, even exemplary. But I guess many readers prefer the writer to repeat himself. I'm pretty sensitive on this point. I have consciously and conscientiously striven to write in different styles, adjusting style to subject at times, other times simply exploring. If the poet is good enough, the voice and the character come through anyhow. The period in which I was writing the poems in *Night Light* was a period when American poets, at least those of my generation who had been writing in the metres, began to jump ship or to surrender their position to the wilder and more experimental writers, who proved themselves expert not just at self-promotion but at polemics as well. Louis

Simpson and James Wright are two very good poets who switched allegiances, partly under the call to arms of Robert Bly. It did seem a time when one was called upon to join up or risk being badly treated – a social force was involved as much as an aesthetic. Well, I was trying to expand my range as well, but without choosing to salute the new order.

I'd like to ask you about the syllabics, if I may. You had used them before, I know, but was Michael Ryan right to conjecture that the development of your interest in the form – 'For the Suicides of 1962', 'The Tourist from Syracuse', 'Hands', 'In the Greenroom', 'At a Rehearsal of Uncle Vanya', and 'To The Hawks' are just some of the syllabic poems in this book – derived from the French poetry you'd been reading, and some of which you'd been translating, in the early Sixties? Or would I be right in thinking that the success which other English-speaking poets had had with the form – amongst them, your old friends Henri Coulette and W.D. Snodgrass – played an important part?

I was interested in syllabics long before translating from French, dating back at least to my first exposure to *In Defence of Reason*, twenty years before *Night Light*. 'To Satan in Heaven', from *The Summer Anniversaries*, was written in the summer of 1952, and is in ten-syllable lines which don't turn into blank verse. Besides, almost none of the French poets I attempted to translate were still writing syllabic lines. Coulette and Snodgrass – not to mention J.V. Cunningham – offered beautiful examples of syllabics in English. Many of us were trying them out, sometimes as an alternative to the accentual-syllabics that were coming under attack.

A note appended to 'At a Rehearsal of Uncle Vanya' tells us that the rehearsal in question was one of those held at the Actor's Workshop in San Francisco in 1964. 'In the Greenroom' has no such explanatory note appended to it, but presumably it could have?

'In the Greenroom' deals with no specific incident but is more generalized; it uses backstage as a kind of metaphor. Of course, it stems from the same period as the Vanya poem, similar circumstances, and I think some of the lines may even have been leftovers from the Vanya poem. It was *Uncle Vanya* the Actor's Workshop was putting on, and 'In the Greenroom' contains an intended reference to *The Cherry Orchard*: 'The sound of the axe / Biting the wood'. Thus it should come across as generalized Chekhov, not too specific. Mike Ryan and others don't seem to like my short five-syllable lines, but I've always thought the five-syllable line had in it a wonderful lyric quality – I would almost call it musical but that, as you know, I don't like to apply that term to poems.

Chekhov is a writer I know you hold in very high esteem. There's a short and rather moving entry in one of the notebooks you excerpted for Oblivion, *which reads as follows: 'A copy of Chekhov's stories lying open on a table. I realized all at once how glad I was that this man had lived. And that I did right to be glad. Of what writers now could that honestly and simply be said?'*

I hold Chekhov in very high esteem, yes, even when he is not quite at his best. One learns to like everything certain writers write. Well, almost everything.

I mentioned your translations from the French a little earlier. Contemporary French Poetry, *an anthology you co-edited with Alexander Aspel, had been published in 1965. It contained translations from the work of fourteen French poets, including a handful by you. How had that anthology come about?*

The anthology was not my idea. Doing it was a job more or less dropped in my lap by Paul Engle. Paul was my boss and had always been very kind to me. I believe he had negotiated a book contract with a press and wanted someone to carry out his project. I couldn't say no. Despite my very modest French, I was stuck with it. The Aspels, Alex and his wife Paulène, herself a poet writing in French, chose the poets included; I was supposed to ask poets who had been at the Iowa Workshop to undertake the translation of a poem or two. If they didn't have much French, they were provided with trots. It was a hit or miss affair. I did not enjoy it. Some of the French poets who knew English – whether much or little it was sometimes hard to say – objected to details of the translations of their poems and turned them into something only approximating English; I had to mediate. Headaches galore. I ended up liking almost nothing about the book, including the French originals. Jacottet and Bonnefoy, along with Char, were surely among the best, but somehow they didn't get to me.

Night Light *contains two poems – 'The Man Closing Up' and 'Hands' – which, though not translations, are inspired by poems of Eugène Guillevic, a French poet with whose work I know you were very taken. Can you say what its appeal was? I think it fair to say that his work has found less of an audience here than that of his contemporaries, Bonnefoy and Jacottet, although his long poem,* Carnac, *translated by John Montague, came out to good reviews here last year.*

Guillevic was for me the exception to what I was just saying. I liked his work, partly because, along with Follain's, it was far less pretentious and arty than the work of most of the poets we were trying to deal with. There was a kind of blunt factuality about it, a concern sometimes with small everyday things, that I respected. He made me think – just a little – of a Frenchified Dr Williams. But in fact he sounded like no American writer and, for that matter, like no other French poet I had come across. Even then, thirty odd years ago, people who kept up with contemporary French poetry told me that Guillevic was hardly one of the more respected contemporaries, and of course they were right. But that didn't matter. The originality I believed I found in his poems had to do in part with the feeling in them, which seemed remarkably warm and humane compared to a sort of French iciness in some of the other poets; but even more with the style, which was spare. I thought it would be interesting to try to bring something of that style over into English – something beyond translation. I believe I succeeded in doing that in 'The Man Closing Up'. But nobody seemed to care. Maybe they were right.

You mentioned William Carlos Williams just now. He's another writer you hold in high esteem, but as Jim Campbell pointed out in his BTL interview with Thom Gunn, he is still regarded a little uneasily over here. The early poems aren't found troublesome, of course, and some – 'To Waken an Old Lady', and 'The 'Widow's Lament in Springtime', for example – are even praised. But by the time of Spring and All, *when Williams's enjambing becomes more frequent, and its rationale correspondingly less obvious, the poems are beginning to irk, and even lead to outbursts like Donald Davie's, who, when reviewing the* Collected Poems *back in 1987, called its author 'the most embarrassing poet in the language,' and 'a dumb ox in American poetry.' What advice would you give to a reader who is baffled by Williams, but who is open to being persuaded that your estimate of him is a fairer one than Davie's?*

First, one must give up any thought that Williams wants to sound like anyone else – anyone else in the history of poetry, including Whitman – or that he *should* sound like anyone else. And this would go double for anyone or anything British, and especially Eliot, who seemed like a turncoat to Williams, a literary traitor. I think he was like a throwback to the early 19th century, to a period when the strongest American writers often seemed desperate to establish their literary independence from England. The two beautiful little poems you mention are early and – I think this is significant – in short lines, like Whitman's only in being seemingly lawless. Short-line free verse was rare, mostly associated with experimental little magazines like *Others*. The very shortness of the lines makes the reasons for division into lines less apparent; in fact most of the time the reasons are not apparent at all, whimsical, perhaps non-existent. Chief among the apparent reasons is simply the desire in Williams to break the line against syntax, not with it, as Stevens was doing with his own short-line free verse at the same time. Williams's theories of metrics seem to me vague and confused, or at least confusing, and I think one would do well not to take them too seriously, though they were certainly intended seriously – anything to be different, to be new, to be personal. I don't think *Spring and All* (which was being written in 1922, the year of *The Waste Land* and *Ulysses*) is a turning point; if anything it seems an extension of his own earlier practice, a further development. Improvisation, or the impression of improvisation, speaking spontaneously, without prior planning, and thus honestly – that, too, is a part of the Williams method. Later – in the Thirties – the early fire seems damped; and I would strongly disagree with those who, like Jarrell, considered *Paterson*, especially its first book, his great achievement. Nor do I think the last phase of his work, beginning with 'The Descent' and featuring his triadic stanza pattern (his 'variable foot') compares well with his work of the Teens and Twenties. Among the late work, I most admire the very late sequence, 'Pictures from Breughel' – poems once more in the short line. Is it just that I prefer him in his least ambitious moments? As for Davie, such venom drips unaccountably from these remarks – one would be stretching the point to call it literary criticism – that the most likely conclusion to be drawn is just that, for some reason, Davie was sadly embittered. As Jarrell remarked of others who did not care for Williams, they 'just twitched as if flies were crawling over them.' Anyone who, like Davie, could prefer Basil Bunting to Williams must be treated with a certain scepticism. My remarks, I fear, will convince nobody, nor would a long and well-thought-out essay, which in any case I don't want to take on. Let's just let it go at this. My advice to the willing reader is to read Williams for pleasure and certainly not for theory. If after trying thirty or forty of the short poems you have found nothing to like, better give up; it's hopeless.

What lay behind your decision to leave Iowa and go to Syracuse in 1966, the year after Contemporary French Poetry, *and the year before* Night Light? *From this vantage point, Iowa – boasting as it does a dozen or more Pulitzer prize winners, three Poet Laureates, and any number of National Book Award and other major literary prize winners – would seem to have been an ideal setting for you. Were you just restless? You'd been in the Midwest for nine years, I know.*

Iowa was an exciting place to be in those days, all right, but I felt that I had been treated unfairly. Several times in my academic life I have felt that and each time I have left. I guess that is about the same thing as being restless.

Well, it might lead to it, but it's surely not the same thing as restlessness. What did or didn't happen, to make you feel you were being treated unfairly?

Let's say there had been an attempt to compromise the independence of the Writers' Workshop, in which I taught, to bring it under the sway and power of the academic side of the English Department – and this would have been disastrous. In any case, hard feelings were bristling all around, and I didn't feel like taking part in any academic (or aesthetic) struggle. There were also questions about money, paltry enough but meaningful all the same.

Anyway, I wasn't just getting away from Iowa, I was attracted by Syracuse, which had an appealing faculty of writers – Delmore Schwartz, George P. Elliott, Philip Booth, and, just a little later, De Snodgrass. As it happened, Schwartz, strangely, never showed up to teach that year, never showed up again at the university. I never met this poet who had been one of the heroes of my youth.

You went back to Iowa in 1971, after a year spent as Visiting Professor at the University of California at Irvine. More restlessness?

I suppose so.

The following year, John Berryman committed suicide by jumping from the Washington Avenue Bridge in Minneapolis. Had you stayed in touch with him over the years?

The year I taught at Hamline University, which was in St Paul, Minnesota, just across the river from the University of Minnesota, where Berryman was teaching, we saw each other now and again. Later, though remaining devoted friends, we never developed much of a correspondence. I had last seen him in the spring of 1966.

Were you surprised by the news of his suicide?

I shouldn't have been surprised, but I was – surprised and shaken. I wrote a poem, since lost. Years later, when in Minneapolis, I walked across the bridge – slowly. That was it.

As a matter of fact, that poem, like your MA thesis, does survive. I've even been able to get hold of a copy. You called it 'Dream Song #309 (posthumous)', and, as the title suggests, it's written in the manner of one of Berryman's eighteen-liners:

> I see here by the papers where it say
> Another American poet's taken flight
> And – zoom! – though on more broken wing by far
> Flies odd feet farther than the Brothers Wright.

Nobody wé acquainted with? – Alas,
You know him well.
Croaks upwards from the Mississippi mud
Henry Frog: C'est moi! – moving on,
As promised, quotes (translated from the prose
Of Monsieur Blah): Who knows
But that the thing afflicting us may be
The secret beginning of some future joy.

'Ain't so. Life
Like a balky elevator
Wasting betwéen floors onetime did
Trap us so seared & close & lonely, seems like,
If you knew.' – I know, Mr Bones, I know.
Somebody punches a button & we go.

Why 'Dream Song #309'?

The title page of *His Toy, His Dream, His Rest* announces 308 poems. I must have meant to imply that my #309 might be added to that number.

Your next collection, Departures, *came out in 1973. You had changed publishers, though, going to Atheneum. Why was that?*

Harry Ford was the poetry editor at Atheneum, and I had met him through Mark Strand. Harry asked for my next book, and I was very happy to give it to him. He was a great editor. At Wesleyan the procedure for having a book taken was much more complicated. You had to please a committee, always an impractical and often an unpleasant system. And it was felt that Atheneum, a commercial publisher rather than an academic press, got a little more notice and respect.

I'll ask you to say some more about Harry Ford later. For the moment, I'd like to stay with Departures. *Bruce Bawer said the same thing about that book as he did about its predecessor, namely that it was an experimental volume, not unaccomplished, but nevertheless falling some way short of the standard set by* The Summer Anniversaries. *In support of this, he even refers to 'The Telephone Number of the Muse', taking it to be an admission that inspiration had deserted you and still not returned:*

> *I call her up sometimes, long distance now.*
> *And still she knows my voice, but I can hear,*
> *Beyond the music of her phonograph,*

The laughter of the young men with their keys.
I have the number written down somewhere.

As I see it, reading this poem as Bawer does is on a par with reading 'Early Poems' as we saw it read earlier on, for, just as 'Early Poems' exemplified the qualities it appears to disparage, so 'The Telephone Number of the Muse' exemplifies the quality it purports to lack.

Bruce Bawer has been a sympathetic reader of my poems, but I hope your reading of 'The Telephone Number of the Muse' is the right one. It certainly is the one intended. One seems not to be permitted to write with tongue in cheek. What is said is too often taken at face value, especially when it involves self-deprecation. Among other things, I was trying to be funny.

'Experimental' is perfectly in order as a description of at least some of the poems in this book, since as you pointed out in a note appended to your Selected Poems *of 1980, 'The Confession', 'The Success', 'The Assassination', and the two sonatinas owe something to your employment of chance operations. You've described these elsewhere, but for the sake of readers who won't have come upon the descriptions, can I ask you to explain them once more, if only briefly?*

I've been asked so many times about my use of 'chance', let me just quote a description of it from an earlier interview. I would 'make up three large decks of 'vocabulary' cards – one deck each for nouns, verbs and adjectives – and a smaller fourth deck of 'syntax' cards, sentence forms with part-of-speech blanks to be filled in. I would then shuffle and deal out a sequence of 'syntax' cards, then shuffle the 'vocabulary' cards in their turn and fill the syntactical blanks in. I would go through all this three times, allowing myself to go back and forth as I wished across the table of results, mixing them up to taste ... And there was enough choice left for the writer's sensibility to enter. I thought that was important.' The process was no doubt 'experimental', though the handful of poems I wrote using this method don't end up sounding much like it, probably because of the final conscious control I kept over the whole business.

I understand that it was after you'd got to know John Cage – he was composer in residence at the University of Cincinnati when you gave your Elliston Lectures there, in 1967 – that you started to use these operations. I take it this wasn't a coincidence?

No coincidence, but no aesthetic ideology whatever involved. My fooling around with 'chance' was like a game, in no way a statement.

Philip Booth remembers a conversation he had with you after your return from Cincinnati, and mentions your talking about your 'working friendship with John Cage'. Did you and he work on anything together?

I don't remember using the phrase. In any case, Cage and I never thought of collaborating — we were much too far apart aesthetically. All the same, he was a fine companion, always cheerful, always interesting.

Do you have any time for his music — if not the wholly aleatory pieces, then at least early pieces like the Sonatas and Interludes?

Not really. Most of it I don't know. While in Cincinnati we did attend together a performance of an early string quartet of his. When it was finished and I praised the piece, which was pretty conservative, he said, all the while smiling and accepting compliments, that he did not care for the piece. It may have been that afternoon that he told me he would rather be a poet than a composer. I said I felt just the reverse of that.

He did try his hand at poetry, didn't he?

> I have nothing to say
> and I am saying it   and that is
> poetry.

On the strength of lines like those, one might even suppose that he had quite a lot of influence as a poet.

No doubt. But no one I've blundered across keeps it as simple as Cage did.

Events of political significance have sometimes moved you to write. Night Light, for example, contained 'To the Hawks', a poem whose date (February, 1965) makes it reasonable to suppose that it was prompted by Johnson's decision to send combat troops to Vietnam. And in Departures there is 'The Assassination', whose date (June 5, 1968) tells anyone for whom the internal clues aren't strong enough that it was prompted by the killing of Robert Kennedy. But if political events have sometimes moved you to write, you are not a political poet, and I imagine that you'd be very sympathetic to the claim, made by the Scottish poet Robert Crawford a few years back, that '[a]s far as politics is concerned, the poet's most important work is to fiddle while Rome burns.'

Most poets would agree with that sentiment. 'Important' may not be the exact word here, but at any rate the poet's work, important or not, is poems.

A handful of poets, especially those temperamentally suited to satire, had done a good job of the political poem. I'm not inclined that way myself. I have just about managed to forget ever having written 'To the Hawks' – just as I have pretty much forgotten the other Vietnam War poems we went around the country reading for a year or two. For me it was a time of giant cosmic fears and a small personal depression.

Was the war much of an issue on the campus at Syracuse, as it was on other campuses across the States?

The usual. All or most of it sincere and impassioned – and not wrong. But some of the people on both sides were unpleasant enough.

There's a fine essay on you by Dana Gioia called 'Tradition and an Individual Talent'. This examines a feature of your writing that had become pretty well established by the time of Departures *– the habit of taking bits and pieces from the work of other writers and using them as starting points for many of your own poems. We saw a fine example earlier on, when you pointed out the 'The Wall''s origins in Shapiro's poem, 'The Sickness of Adam'. 'The Wall' does exactly what Gioia says you're able to do when you borrow in this way, and 'coaxes a new poem out of the unrealized possibilities suggested by a borrowed phrase or image.' Gioia compares and contrasts this practice of yours with that of literary forebears such as Pound, Eliot and Moore, and what he says is very illuminating. However, I'm not sure that his discussion doesn't miss a trick or two. To begin with, if it's literary forebears he's looking for, I think a more profitable comparison is likely to be with Weldon Kees. I didn't read Henry James's* The American Scene *until very recently – led to it by a sequence of yours that I'll want to discuss separately a little later on – but about halfway through the book I encountered 'The Sense of Newport', and was instantly reminded of Kees's poem, 'Henry James at Newport', which turns out, on close examination, to be a versification of extracts from that very book:*

> And shores and strands and naked piers,
> Sunset on waves, orange laddering the blue,
> White sails on headlands, cool
> Wide curving bay, dim landward distances
> Dissolving in the property of local air ...

At the very least, I take it this poem was an encouragement to you?

But at the time I came to do my version of James I'd forgotten the Kees poem. I mean consciously. Some of my infamous borrowings no doubt stem from this doubtful memory of mine.

Then let me come to the other thing I wanted to ask in connection with Gioia's article, which is whether, in concentrating on your literary forebears, he isn't overlooking something of significance. You have often been asked whether your musical background hasn't influenced your writing in any way, and in general have been quite dismissive of the idea – understandably, given the silly things that have often been said about music and verse. But wouldn't it be right to see one of the important ways in which you take off from the work of others as owing more to a musical than a literary tradition?

Do you mean the sounds, especially the metres, of other poems? If so, I'm not conscious of such borrowings.

No, that's not what I mean, although I can think of one instance where you borrow a metre – in 'Counting the Mad'. No, I'm talking about the very same things as Gioia: images (like the angel's unfurling wings in 'The Wall'), words (like the teleutons in your Kees sestina), phrases (like those you weave into 'The Tourist from Syracuse'), whole sentences (like the ones you use in 'Young Girls Growing Up'). The practice reminds me of the ways in which composers take figures, themes or whole passages from the works of other composers, and then write variations on them.

Well, of course, doing variations on the work of others is a venerable and honourable tradition in painting as well as in music. Van Gogh's use of Millet springs to mind as one example. A form of *hommage.*

I'm sure one can find examples in all of the arts – in painting and sculpture, obviously, but in fiction, architecture, and film as well. However, the practice does seem to be better established in music than it does in these other fields – there'll be an entry for it in most encyclopaedias or dictionaries of music, but not in most encyclopaedias or dictionaries of the other arts. Moreover, music was something you'd been immersed in from an early age.

You've convinced me.

Three or four pages of Stephen Dobyns's Best Words, Best Order *are devoted to a formal analysis of the last-but-one poem in* Departures, *'Absences'. Dobyns's discussion is very interesting, but it makes me want to ask a naïve-sounding question, a question it may make more sense to put to an habitual reviser like yourself than to the sort of poet whose first drafts are very often their last. What I'd like to know is how much of what's going on formally in your poems – many of which would require a good deal more than three or*

61

four pages of analysis to uncover – you are conscious of, and consciously manipulating?

I'm conscious of some. But I have been surprised several times by what others have discovered – or read into – something I've written in all innocence. Sometimes I like what is uncovered; sometimes I doubt that it's there. My favourite discoveries of this kind are the ones Robert Mezey finds in a small essay of his called 'Of Donald Justice's Ear'. The effects he finds are beyond my conscious powers and I was unaware of them until I read his piece. I can only hope he's right.

A little earlier, we talked about your Ford Fellowship, but I allowed myself to get side-tracked. Could we come to your work for the stage, just for a moment?

Of course.

During the late Seventies, you adapted something of Eudora Welty's for the stage. But I'm a little puzzled about what it was. According to the University of Delaware's on-line index of your papers, it was an 'adaptation of [her] short story, "The Golden Apples"', and was entitled 'The Whole World Knows'. But there is clearly something wrong with this description, because 'The Golden Apples', or, rather, The Golden Apples, isn't a short story, it's a cycle of short stories, of which 'The Whole World Knows' is just one. My first thought was that you must have adapted that one story, but after reading it I thought that very unlikely. More recently I've seen a copy of the letter Ms Welty wrote to the Dramatists' Guild, seeking advice about the terms on which she should give you the go-ahead: 'Enclosed are Xerox copies of a letter to me from Mr Donald Justice, of Iowa City, who has written an adaptation of some stories of mine and has already shown it to Mr Dan Mason of Shelter West who wants to do an off-off Broadway production.' This strongly suggests, what I would in any case have suspected, that you adapted incidents from several of the stories in that cycle.

Those Welty adaptations were for a form of dramatization called in those days – the early Seventies – Readers' Theatre. As I recall, there were three of them: 'The Whole World Knows', 'The Hitchhikers' (my two favourite Welty stories) and 'Keela, the Outcast Indian Maiden'. Only one of the three came from The Golden Apples. As far as the correspondence you've seen – I don't have any recollection of ever having seen the Welty letter. She did write a very polite letter to me suggesting that correspondence regarding the plays should be directed to her agent; this was enough to discourage my rather fragile hopes. I would have been happy for Mr Mason, whom I did not know, to do a production, but I remember no negotiations that might have led to a performance.

So the adaptations never got their 'off-off Broadway' production?

No.

Did they get produced anywhere else?

None achieved production, even locally – which I regret. Nor will they, I guess.

Did Ms Welty get to see what you'd done with her stories?

I don't believe Ms Welty saw anything but my inquiring letter. I don't believe she'd have wanted to see anything else, and who could blame her for that? – But you amaze me by how much you know about something I thought had been completely forgotten – nay, lost.

Your Selected Poems *came out in 1979, and the following spring you were rewarded with the Pulitzer Prize for Poetry. How much of an effect do you think that had on your career?*

I was offered a couple of jobs and invited to do a few more readings. By those who knew little of poetry I was treated with more interest, more respect.

The Selected *contained sixteen previously uncollected poems, including 'Childhood', a luminous evocation of the Miami in which you grew up.*

> And there are
> Colognes that mingle on the barber's hands
> Swathing me in his striped cloth, Saturdays, downtown.
> Billy, the midget haberdasher, stands grinning
> Under the winking neon goat, his sign,
> As Flagler's sidewalks fill. Slowly
> The wooden escalator rattles upward
> Toward the twin fountains of the mezzanine
> Where boys, secretly brave, prepare to taste
> The otherness trickling there, forbidden ...
>
> And then the warm cashews in cool arcades!

O counters of spectacles! — where the bored child first
Scans new perspectives squinting through strange lenses;
And the mirrors, tilting, offer back toy sails
Stiffening breezeless toward green shores of baize ...

Rather than ask you about the poem itself, I'd like to ask you about the notes you wrote for it ...

Well, as the lines you've quoted show, the poem contains a number of references to things with which very few readers would be familiar. In fact, I can think of only one other survivor who would qualify, and he is not in good health. It seemed to me that some identification was necessary. Since I believe in a poetry based on reality and simple truth, I believed the facts of the poem – which in their own stubborn way worked like or seemed to become images – would be enhanced if their sources were known. That's why I wrote the notes.

I understand that, but in the Selected *the notes were printed alongside the poem – as Crane had laid out his notes for* The Bridge, *and as Coleridge had laid out his for 'The Ancient Mariner' – yet by the time 'Childhood' was reprinted in your New and Selected Poems of 1995 – it was from the later, slightly revised version that I was quoting just now – the notes were no longer on the same page, but had taken their place with those that appeared at the end of the book. I'm curious to know why you first printed them the one way and then printed them the other.*

I was indeed thinking of Crane and Coleridge when I started out; for a long time I had wished for an occasion that might evoke such magnificent marginalia as theirs. I wasted many hours trying to approach the beauty and grandeur of their marginalia. But my prose notes would not take off; they remained nothing more than footnotes hoping to preserve some ancient and vanished civilization. In the end I thought they deserved no more space and attention than footnotes – there for the curious but forced upon no one.

You're the second of our interviewees who appears, as himself, in a novel. The first was Michael Hamburger, who figures in W.G. Sebald's 1995 novel, The Rings of Saturn. Your turn had come rather earlier, with John Irving's 1981 novel, The Hotel New Hampshire. 'Love's Stratagems' and 'On the Death of Friends in Childhood' are quoted entire, and lines from 'The Summer Anniversaries', 'But That is Another Story', 'Men at Forty', 'The Tourist from Syracuse' and 'The Evening of the Mind' are also scattered about. I take it you've read the book?

Yes, but I don't recall all the references to poems you've found. Reading the novel, I must have missed some. But how could one be anything but pleased by such attention? Apparently, the director of the movie, Tony Richardson, was never aware that the character bearing my name was a real person – at any rate, the couple of lines quoted in the movie were not credited. A few weeks after the release of the movie I received a phone call from someone – John Irving's agent, I believe it was – offering to recompense me for the oversight. The Wesleyan Press dealt with the question and, as far as I can recall, split a $500 fee with me – the most I ever got for a couple of lines of poetry.

How did it feel, encountering yourself in Irving's novel, a poet whose work is so admired by the narrator's sister that, knowing she'll never be able to reach your standard – 'Damn that Donald Justice, anyway! He's written all the good lines!' – she ends up taking her own life?

That was too much even for me, but it was an important part of the story, I figure.

Did you get to know Irving in Iowa? He studied there, I know, and taught there for a while.

I didn't know him when he was studying there. Kurt Vonnegut was his teacher, I think. Later, when we were both on the faculty, we saw a little of one another. But it wasn't till we were both teaching at the Bread Loaf summer conference that we became friends.

You've written under a number of pseudonyms down the years: Rodney Cook, Vasco Lee, Orville St John, and – my favourite – Manfred Stonesifer. What motive or motives had you for engaging in these subterfuges?

I don't remember the name Manfred Stonesifer at all. If I should ever use a pseudonym again, though, that would be my first choice, now that you mention it.

But we'll have let the cat out of the bag with this interview.

I suppose so. But how in the world did you get wind of all this? For me it's something like reading an FBI report on one's suspicious activities.

Between The Lines goes behind them when it has to!

But you were asking about my motives for using these pseudonyms, and here I can tell you an interesting story. I've often written poems that aren't, as I see them, quite worth acknowledging, but which at the same time seem as good as, and usually better than, the poems I read in the literary magazines. I wonder if a lot of writers don't feel that way. Anyhow, I thought I would test the discernment of editors, and the test would be tougher if my name weren't attached. The upshot was that I sent poems out under an array of names, perhaps a little more than a dozen poems all told, and all totally without result. Served me right, I don't doubt. One editor did scribble something like 'Try us again' on the rejection notice. I'd had better luck at sixteen in getting such consoling encouragements. I became increasingly embarrassed – both for myself and for the editors at large, who seemed to me so woefully mistaken but who in some cases had been all along publishing poems signed with my real name. Was it the name that counted?

Did you go on to submit any of these poems under your own name? If so, what happened?

I did revise one extensively – the John Lenox Bassoonist poem – and it was accepted immediately with my name on it. Admittedly it was better in its revised state, but I like to think ... No, I don't want to stray off on that tangent.

In 1982 you left the University of Iowa, to take up a post at the University of Florida at Gainesville. William Logan, a former student of yours, has said that when he received an invitation to direct the writing program there, he had his misgivings: 'Florida was everything I disliked about the South – too hot, too provincial, too sandy, too racist. The only attractions were the alligators and the Justices.' For you, though, I take it this was a kind of homecoming, with rather more than alligators to offer?

Yes, it seemed at first like a homecoming. That was before the theorists took over the department – a period I think of as the invasion of the body snatchers. But in the first few years I was still able to preserve my naïve illusion that coming back to Florida was exactly what a benign fate had had in store for me – even though this was the cracker Florida of William Logan's apprehensions and not the Miami of the past, my own very different Florida. I have a distinct memory of walking out onto the golf course behind our house late one night, walking our dog, and standing there looking up at the moon as it flooded the fairway with light. Very nice. I felt touched by an emotion I must have been inventing.

1984 saw the publication of Platonic Scripts, *which gathered together a number of your critical essays – including fine pieces like 'Baudelaire: The*

Question of His Sincerity; or Variations on Several Texts by Eliot', 'Metres and Memory', and 'The Free-Verse Line in Stevens' – as well as a number of the interviews you had given since the mid-Sixties. Its preface opens with the following words: 'Of all the poets of my generation who did not get much into the habit of criticism – and that would include the great majority of us – I may be the only one with any regrets at having kept my thoughts more or less to myself. I see now that criticism can be of enormous value in helping to define and refine one's own thinking; and there is always the chance, if it is any good, that it might do the same for another's.' Why was it that so few of your generation really bothered with writing criticism? One might have expected that a group of people whose teachers included so many noted poet-critics wouldn't have needed any prodding.

I may be wrong about this, but lately I have come to believe that the time we had for writing criticism was used instead for writing polemics, in some cases polemics masquerading as criticism. Robert Bly is the perfect example of this. That kind of thinking dominated the scene for too long, in my opinion. The simpler explanation might just be that, preceded, as we were, by a host of first-rate critics, we felt there was not much left to say along those lines. But I shouldn't be speaking for others. I expect we all would have agreed that writing poems was in any case somehow more glorious than tossing off critical essays.

Is criticism something you can write during a period when you're also writing poetry?

Sure.

You don't find the habits and dispositions required by each activity inhospitable to each other?

You can be writing several things, several kinds of things, at once. No problem.

Would you say that being a poet is a necessary condition of being a critic, or a good critic, at any rate? I ask because each of the critics to whom Oblivion is dedicated was also a poet – Blackmur, Eliot, Empson, Ransom, Tate and Winters.

I would say that being a poet is a necessary condition of being a critic of poetry, though the professional critic does not think so.

If we delve back into the nineteenth, eighteenth and seventeenth centuries,

I suspect your case is going to look even stronger, what with Arnold, Col-eridge, Wordsworth, Johnson, Dryden, Milton, Jonson – poet-critics all. Still, I wonder if regarding it as a necessary condition isn't a mistake ...

An idea just popped into my head: let every aspiring critic of poetry be required to publish his or her poems before being allowed to do criticism. Not that writing bad poems would disqualify the would-be critic; only that we would have direct evidence of the sensibility involved and therefore a good basis for determining whether we wanted to listen to the criticism be-ing offered. But there really is no necessary correlation, I suppose, between the value of the criticism and the poetry. Blackmur is the least successful poet among the figures you listed, but a more appealing critic than some of the others.

But I think that makes my point, because it concedes that the best evidence of a critic's sensibility isn't necessarily to be found in any poetry they may write, but in their criticism. Would we have had better evidence of Gom-brich's sensibility as an art critic if we'd made him sit a test in painting? Or of Shaw's sensibility as a music critic if we'd made him sit a test in composi-tion? Of course, Gombrich loves art, just as Shaw loved music, and I wonder if what lies behind your suggestion that people be required to publish po-ems before being allowed to do criticism is the conviction that today's liter-ary critics write what they do out of a sentiment quite removed from love.

The test seemed like such a good idea, but I can see that you're right.

I mentioned Shaw just now. Reviewing the three volumes of his music criti-cism a few years ago, Charles Rosen declared that 'being right does not matter very much in music criticism: almost anybody can be right. What counts is the basis for judgement. No doubt, if the ideas that go into the making of an evaluation, the point of view that illuminates it and the reason-ing that justifies it are persuasive and lively, the criticism remains valid even when one rejects the final judgement.' Would you go along with that? And if so, can an analogous claim be made about literary criticism?

No, I wouldn't go along. It's an important function of criticism – in all of the arts, not just in music – to evaluate, to pass judgement. And the obligation to be right ought to be felt. Not that one can always hope to *be* right. It could be argued that it is also important to be right for the right reasons – a view closer to Rosen's, I suppose. Good, firm principles *ought* to work for good evalua-tions but should not be trusted too far – they become very bendable.

Your next collection, The Sunset Maker, *was published in 1987. If Frost was right about poems being stays against confusion, then the poems in this book are stays against a particular variety of confusion, the variety we associate with loss. The same can be said about earlier poems, of course, but the autumnal quality of this book taken as a whole is unprecedented. As well as the poems,* The Sunset Maker *contains three pieces of prose – a memoir and two short stories – and the impulse behind these is just the same. You're battling against 'the formless ruin of oblivion'. Would this collection have been significantly different if you'd not gone back to Florida, do you think? Or would the approach of your sixtieth birthday have ensured a book much like this, regardless of where you were living?*

The thought had never occurred to me, but almost certainly the book would have been different. Very different. Probably gloomier. I'm thinking of subject matter, not technique.

You were fifty-seven years old when you returned to Florida, thirty or so years after it had ceased to be your home. Henry James was only a few years older than that when he returned to America, twenty or so years after it had ceased to be his home. Presumably it was because of what you saw to be the parallels that you chose to versify extracts from James's Notebooks *and* The American Scene, *producing 'American Scenes (1904-1905)'?*

Parallels? I don't know about that. The James book is in its own eccentric way so irresistible that one day I just began to tinker with some of the beautiful baroque sentences to see how readily they would adapt to verse, to rhyme and metre. Pretty easily, I found – and began dashing off little passages drawn from the Jamesian prose, of which the ones I printed seemed to me the best.

The four parts of 'American Scenes (1904-1905)' deal, respectively, with James's time in Cambridge, Massachusetts, Richmond, Virginia, Charleston, South Carolina, and Coronado Beach, California. Why, I wonder, wasn't there a fifth part, dealing with his stay in Florida, the state to which you had only recently returned, and which he called 'the softest lap the whole South had to offer', whose 'softness was divine – like something mixed, in a huge silver crucible, as an elixir, and then liquidly scattered'?

As a matter of fact, I did write a fifth part about Florida, and what is left of it can be found buried in one of the notebook sections of *Oblivion*:

> Here was the Infinite Previous, an age
> When nothing yet was set down on the page,
> A plate too primitive for all our inks.
> A Nile before the Pharaoh or the Sphinx.

For months I thought of Florida – the state in which I had been born and brought up as the Infinite Previous. An absolutely brilliant phrase.

The book is teeming with brilliant phrases. It's no wonder you were drawn to it.

And other poets since. Joe Bolton, whose posthumous volume, *The Last Nostalgia,* I edited in 1999, also wrote a poem based on *The American Scene,* and I have heard that the poet Debora Greger has occasionally given her students an assignment to versify something from the book.

Which one of Bolton's poems were you referring to just now?

It's a beautiful sonnet entitled 'Florida Twilight, 1905':

> Returning late, the flushed West to the right,
> One saw, aligned against the golden sky
> (The very throne-robe of the star-crowned night),
> Black palms, a frieze of chiselled ebony.
> And even at the moment one resolved
> Not to come back, the scent of fruit and flowers
> Brought on a sadness as the past dissolved:
> Arcades, courts, arches, fountains, lordly towers ....
>
> The shore of sunset and the palms, meanwhile –
> Late shade giving over to greater shade –
> What were they? With what did they have to do?
> It was like myriad pictures of the Nile.
> But with a History yet to be made,
> A world already lost that was still new.

Now I understand where the title of his book comes from. The section of James's book from which the borrowed phrases in this poem are taken is called 'The Last Regret'.

That's right.

Your poems often focus on a gesture or action of some sort, and the manner in which they do this strikes me as cinematographic. I'm thinking about such things as the unfurling wings of 'The Wall', the shutting eyes and the wave in 'To the Hawks', and the arms held open in 'The Assassination', or, to come up to date, the outspaced hands in 'Children Walking Home from School through Good Neighbourhood'. Do you see what I'm getting at?

I'd never noticed but, yes, I think you're right. It does sound a bit stagey. Perhaps it comes from a lifelong ambition not only to write plays but to direct them.

I wouldn't call them 'stagey', not for a moment. That suggests something artificial or affected, and what you achieve at such moments is a long way from being either. Each is as right, and as compelling, as, say, the freeze-frame with which Truffaut closes Les Quatres Cents Coups, *or the slow motion sequence with which Roeg gets* Don't Look Now *properly under way. Are you much of a film goer, incidentally? The medium doesn't make too many explicit appearances in your work – 'A Dancer's Life' was inspired by Bergman, I know, and 'Memories of the Depression Years' includes a reference to D.W. Griffith – but my hunch is you're quite keen on the cinema.*

Not only am I a filmgoer – perhaps I should say *used to be,* given the recent movies available on local screens – but like many fans I'd like to think I have a special feel for the movies. Oh, not as keen as our son Nat, who as a kid memorized Sarris's *American Cinema,* out of devotion. Funny that I should have mentioned Bergman and Griffith in poems, since they're by no means favourites of mine. Give me Renoir and Vigo and Ford, and for comedy Preston Sturges, say. Oh, Welles, of course.

In 1991 you won another major prize, the Bollingen, awarded for a lifetime's achievement in poetry. Then, in 1992, after a decade spent teaching at the University of Florida, you retired. According to William Logan, you had grown disaffected, both with Florida and with the university, and so had started to think about leaving even before the mild heart attack you suffered in 1990. You've already indicated what it was about the university that irked you, and I'd be happy if you wished to say more, but to begin with I'd like you to say what it was about the place you didn't care for.

Well, north Florida, where the university is, was not the south Florida of memory. (Neither, of course, would the south Florida of the present be the Florida I remember.) As well, there was a certain nostalgia for the Iowa City of our youth; a certain tug of affection made itself felt. But the real reason for my disaffection had less to do with the place than the university, and especially the English department.

Invaded by the body snatchers.

The theorists, yes – a bloody-minded and unsavoury lot.

Do you know that joke about the theorists? Question: What do you get

71

when you cross a theorist and a mafioso? Answer: *An offer you can't understand.*

I'll try to remember that one. Only the writers and a handful of students had
escaped the curse. My antipathy was so great it did not even occur to me
that, once retired, I would never have to deal with them any more.

*I owe the joke to Jay Parini's essay, 'The Lessons of Theory', which as you
probably know takes creative writers to task for not engaging with the theorists:*

> 'Literary theory – or just "theory" – has frightened a whole gen-
> eration of intellectuals into early mental retirement, mostly be-
> cause they have not had the stamina or will to enter into appro-
> priate conversation with their younger colleagues. Perhaps the
> most unfortunate aspect of the debate over theory has been this
> extension into the academy of what, in the Sixties, used to be
> called the generation gap; indeed, many of the same dynamics
> seem to apply, with theorists pitting themselves against all forms
> of authority. Never trust anyone over thirty has been transmogri-
> fied into never trust anyone who doesn't appreciate Foucault.'

*What do you make of that, as an account of what happened inside your own
and other English departments during the Eighties and Nineties?*

It seems straightforward enough, except for the claim that we who retired
retired mentally, which isn't at all fair. My mental energy kept going well
enough, and on finer projects than debating with people who'd read Foucault
but never looked at Tolstoy. And why should the obligation to enter into
appropriate conversation have rested on us – the good guys – rather than on
them?

*It sounds to me as though you had rather more against them than that they
had read Foucault and not Tolstoy.*

I disliked practically everything about them: their jargon and their grammar,
their vast intellectual pretensions, their easy disdain for things they knew
little or nothing about and had no interest in, their lousy taste in literature
and the other arts, their nasty politicking, their hatred of the past and the
tradition in favour of the fashionable and the perfectly silly ... But please
don't get me wound up. It's been years and I still tremble with passion.

*You are an accomplished artist, as the covers of some recent books – The
Sunset Maker, New and Selected Poems, Oblivion, Orpheus Hesitated Be-*

side the Black River – *reveal. When did you first take up a brush and paints?*

1984 or '85. Around Christmas, it must have been. My wife asked me what I wanted for Christmas and I said – out of what unexplored depths of longing I have no idea – some water-colours. I knew nothing about drawing or painting, nothing whatever, but I did try to teach myself – and found that it gave me more immediate pleasure than writing, though I would always remain an amateur at it.

Well, your publishers think well enough of your efforts, and so too, I believe, did Richard Frost, whose Jazz for Kirby *you illustrated. How did that come about?*

I first asked Harry Ford if he'd consider looking at some of the paintings and drawings I'd just begun doing, with the hope of finding one we could use as a cover. This was for *The Sunset Maker*, and since Harry approved, it turned out to be the first of several books that used work of mine on covers. I'd already done a couple of linocuts of musicians when Dick Frost asked if I had anything he could use on the cover of a chapbook, and I was glad to have a supply on hand.

I believe that you and Mark Strand – another poet who paints, of course – once invented a board-game, modelled on Monopoly, but with works of art rather than property the objects to be collected. My informant tells me that you had everything worked out in elaborate detail: 'a Monet was worth four Dalis, and a Vermeer was among the most costly and desirable items.' Whatever became of this game?

That was years ago, long before I started to paint. But again you have me at a loss. I would have said, if anyone asked, that only Mark and I knew about it.

My source in this case was Tony Hecht.

Well, we never got as far along with it as Tony thought. Our attempts were soon abandoned – it was just too difficult to work it out in detail. But I'd love to give playing it a try, if someone else would do the dirty work of inventing it.

So you and Strand never got as far as discussing, let alone arguing about, the exchange values of your artists?

Had we got as far as discussing them, I am sure I would have yielded automatically to Mark's judgement; he was the acknowledged expert. But no, we never got that far.

Nor to establishing what would have constituted a jailable move?

No, though there would have been a few of considerable interest – forgery and looting, to start with.

It sounds to me like there could have been at least as much fun in devising the game as in playing it.

Possibly, but until you sit down and try to work everything out, you don't realize how difficult it is. We might have been able to solve some of the problems by using fictitious painters, for example, but that would also have eliminated some of the fun.

Given just how devoted you are to the visual arts, I wonder why it is that they haven't figured more often in your poetry? Offhand, I can only think of the following examples: 'Anonymous Drawing', 'On a Painting by Patient B of the Independence State Hospital for the Insane', 'Mule Team and Poster', 'The Sunset Maker' ...

There's the two-liner, 'On a Painting by Burchfield'.

Of course, and 'Sadness' too, whose fourth stanza mentions another painting by the same artist. But this is still a small number, given your love of the visual arts.

One popular notion used to be – still may be, for all I know – that one mustn't write poems about paintings. And this despite the beautiful examples in Snodgrass, for instance, or Williams's Breughel poems, and dozens more.

You mentioned a related notion earlier, when you recalled Shapiro's hostility to poems inspired by literature. It's as though an unlawful liaison were involved, the offspring of which cannot but be enfeebled in some way. You'd never guess just how long and vigorous is the tradition of such liaisons.

In any case, being outlawed as a genre should have made it more appealing to me.

I had to look Burchfield up, never having come across the name before. But now I've tracked him down, and seen some examples of his work – not, I'm afraid, the paintings referred to in your poems – I can understand why you think so highly of him.

Burchfield's not very widely known abroad, but he seems to me to be one of those American originals I mentioned before.

Now might be a good moment at which to ask you about another of the American originals you mentioned earlier – Sherwood Anderson. More people over here will recognize Anderson's name than will recognize Burchfield's, but I had to ring round a number of London bookshops before I could find one that stocked any of his books. What is it about Anderson that so appeals to you?

There's his prose style, so natural, so easy, so full of unforced feeling – and his human sympathy, which is also unforced and quiet, but unmistakable. This is especially true of his masterpiece, *Winesburg, Ohio*, and two or three of his short stories. And it's not only in British book shops that you might have trouble finding Anderson; it's American book shops as well.

This is by the by, but I recently re-read your essay, 'The Prose Sublime: Or the Deep Sense of Things Belonging Together, Inexplicably', which of course devotes a fair amount of space to Anderson's work. And I was taken aback to discover a passage towards the end in which you compare those moments when an author achieves this thing, the prose sublime, to moments 'at which the action, pausing, gives way to a held picture, something like the cinematic freeze-frame or a fermata in music; the picture in itself seems to represent, almost abstractly, some complex of meaning and feeling.' But let us move on. A number of the people you most admire for their achievement in the arts have had more than one string to their artistic bow. Ruggles the composer was a gifted painter, Welty the writer of fiction was a gifted photographer, Kees the poet was not just a painter and a photographer, but a composer, a writer of fiction, a dramatist and a film-maker, and in at least two of those fields was not just gifted but exceptional. I'm reminded of your lines about Madam L., the subject of 'On a Woman of Spirit Who Taught Both Piano and Dance', 'whose heart / Was a hummingbird's, and flew from art to art.'

The coincidence – if that is what it is – I had never noticed before.

You continued to write music over the years. One of the pieces you've finished recently, and which I've been fortunate to hear a live recording of, is Winesburg, a setting for tenor and string trio of nine phrases from what you just called Anderson's masterpiece, Winesburg, Ohio. The phrases you've set are:

> Death, night, the sea, fear, loneliness
> Little puffs of dust arose in the lamp-light
> And then something happened, something happened
> And on summer evenings when the air vibrated with the song of insects
> Only the few know the sweetness of the twisted apples
> Lust, lust, women and night
> On all sides are ghosts, not of the dead, but of living people
> A thing blown by the wind, a thing destined like corn to wilt in the sun
> Then he slept

Can I ask why you chose these phrases?

I wanted brief, evocative, romantic, Andersonian phrases. I jotted down perhaps two dozen of them while thumbing through the book several times. Only the first and last phrases plus the famous 'twisted apples' phrase were certainties from the first. I mean some day to add two or three more phrases; there are plenty of beautiful ones, phrases that seem to fit perfectly into my sensibility, at least my musical sensibility, such as it is. Oh, yes, I should probably mention that the whole idea of the thing began with a short story of mine called 'Ma Non Troppo', later changed to 'Death, Night, Etc.' But I know how very small a part this piece is of the immense world of music – 'a thing blown by the wind.' In spite of which, I'm not sorry to have spent as much of myself as I did on five or six minutes of music. And, as I say, I plan to add more phrases, more fragments.

The fragmentary can have remarkable power. I wonder if this isn't connected with something you say in an interesting passage in 'The Prose Sublime'?

'According to Percy Lubbock, James's great interpreter, the reader of a novel finds it impossible to retain what Lubbock calls "the image of a book" entire. It must be nearly as hard for the author to manage this trick himself. Always, says Lubbock, "the image escapes and evades us like a cloud." Yet it does not entirely escape. In our memory there remains forever some image of the novel called Madame Bovary, and it is not at all the same as the remembered image of War and Peace or The Wings of the Dove. Ours are doubtless only phantasmal images of the whole – we could never, like a Borgesian character, become the true author of any of these novels – but these cloudy images have still enough of the contours of a wholeness about them to enable us to think of each one individually and quite distinctly.

And is wholeness the question anyhow? More vivid and alive, certainly, are those broken-off pieces of the whole which continue to drift across our consciousness more or less permanently, fragments though they are.'

What do you make of the other writers with whom Anderson is usually bracketed? You've already told us what you feel about Sinclair Lewis – your mother's year-long ban on his work was a lesson as much aesthetic as moral or political, so you said – but what about Edgar Lee Masters or Thomas Wolfe?

It's funny you should mention Masters, because I'm presently deeply sunk into his *Spoon River Anthology*. It's a book I'd never liked much before; now, though, I see that there's wonderful stuff in it, if one can just get past all the banality and didacticism. As a matter of fact, I'm so taken with the *Anthology* that I'm thinking of trying to compose a small cantata based on it. The chances are I won't have the staying power, in which case I'll offer the idea to a couple of composer friends of mine. As to Thomas Wolfe – I read him worshipfully as an adolescent, but he's hard going now.

Is artistic collaboration something you find easy?

Yes, I think so, except, come to think of it, with my old friend Dick Stern. We got through the first speech of a play we were going to attempt and couldn't agree on the second speech – so ended the collaboration.

After retiring from the University of Florida, you moved back to Iowa City, where you've lived ever since. You've published A Donald Justice Reader *(1992),* New and Selected Poems *(1995),* Orpheus Hesitated Beside the Dark River: Poems 1952-1997 *(1998), and a second collection of critical essays,* Oblivion *(1998). There've also been editions of other poets' work, which I'll ask you to say more about in a moment. It doesn't seem as though you've found it too difficult filling the time unoccupied by teaching.*

I've been busier than ever, or so it seems. I've heard others say the same. One begins to see that there is simply not going to be enough time to do all the things one wants to do.

A striking thing about A Donald Justice Reader *is its organization, which isn't chronological but thematic. I thought I was going to dislike it – as I dislike the current fashion for thematic rather than chronological hangings in art museums – but in fact I found it very illuminating. Was this your idea, or your editors'?*

I think I was allowed to order the contents in any way I pleased. Academic presses have a tendency to let their authors do most of the work, I believe, which is fine with me. I've never thought the organization of a book of poems mattered very much anyhow, but there I realize I'm in a minority.

The rules governing particular forms are not sacrosanct as far as you are concerned, are they? If I look back, I can find a thirteen-lined sonnet, a three-terceted villanelle, a sestina without an envoi ...

I like to leave a rough spot or two in handling any of the forms, a mark of authenticity, so to speak.

> Such art has nature in her kind
> That in the shaping of a hill
> She will take care to leave behind
> Some few abutments here and there,
> Something to cling to, just in case.
> A taste more finical and nice
> Would comb out kink and curl alike.

That's from an early poem, 'Variations on a Theme from James', and it means to state the case for these rough spots. As you say, the rules are not sacrosanct. In fact, both Hardy and Ransom endorse a certain roughening.

One of the new poems in your New and Selected *was 'Pantoum of the Great Depression', whose first two quatrains go as follows:*

> *Our lives avoided tragedy*
> *Simply by going on and on,*
> *Without end and with little apparent meaning.*
> *Oh, there were storms and small catastrophes.*
>
> *Simply by going on and on*
> *We managed. No need for the heroic.*
> *Oh, there were storms and small catastrophes.*
> *I don't remember all the particulars.*

The speaker is refusing to describe his life as tragic, not because he's like one of those tenant farmers who stare out at us from a Walker Evans photograph – an impoverished yet dignified figure, down but not out – but because he knows what's been said about the nature of tragedy – that it requires heroics, a plot, an ending, etc., – and recognizes that his own life, and the lives of others like him, simply don't qualify.

It's the validity of Aristotle's idea of tragedy for the middle and lower classes that's being questioned, and the poem strongly suggests that the ordinary sufferings of the masses are more important than poetry, even with all its beauties and consolations.

I mentioned this poem not just because I admire it, but because it's another whose form you've 'roughed up'. A pantoum is normally written in quatrains, with certain of its lines repeated or echoed through the stanzas in a fixed pattern. Your 'Pantoum of the Great Depression' seems to be no exception to the rule, until one gets to the end, which coincides not with the last quatrain's last line, but with a single line, which reads as follows:

> And there is no plot in that; it is devoid of poetry.

Can you say something about that last line, which seems to be a close relative of the single line with which your earlier poem, 'Cinema and Ballad of the Great Depression', ends – resembling that, too, in the way it echoes a couple of lines from about halfway through?

For one thing, the last line simply sounds to me more final than the next-to-last line, therefore useful. And then it's a final echo of the *Poetics* of Aristotle. It's these frequent reminders of Aristotelian propositions that serve as a sort of underpinning for the whole poem, the last one being the most summary and dismissive.

A rather different poem about the Depression is 'Banjo Dog Variations', which conjures up the memories of a man who'd been obliged to lead the life of a hobo, hitching rides on freight trains, sleeping under tarpaulins, stopping in towns where men were so desperate that they'd see off rivals for work with baseball bats and iron bars, spending a few days in jail ... But the spirit in which he recalls those years isn't anguished; it's actually rather wistful, in one place quite explicitly so:

> I miss the smell of the ratty furs
> And Saturday night cologne and beer,
> And I miss the juke and the sign that read:
> NO POLICE SERVED HERE.

The Cinema and Ballad poem is simply a first try at the subject; the Banjo Dog poem is the second full try and the last. Before anything else, there had been these now lost lines: 'Reading about the thirties, / I got depressed myself'. The lines popped into my head as I was looking through a wonderful book of period photographs called *A Vision Shared*, put together by Hank

O'Neal in the Seventies. Sadly, I could never work this pair of lines into the bigger poem I had in mind, true though they were.

Why 'Banjo Dog', incidentally?

I found the phrase in a Sherwood Anderson novel, *Dark Laughter*. But you know, I've no idea what a banjo dog is ...

It's not explained in the novel?

No, it occurs as part of a song, with no explanation given:

> 'The words coming from the throats of the black workers could not be understood by the boy but were strong and lovely. Afterwards when he thought of that moment Bruce always remembered the singing voices of the negro deck-hands as colours. Streaming reds, browns, golden yellows coming out of black throats. He grew strangely excited inside himself, and his mother, sitting beside him, was also excited. "Ah, my baby! Ah, my baby!" Sounds caught and held in black throats. Notes split in quarter-notes. The word, as meaning, of no importance. Perhaps words were always unimportant. There were strange words about a "banjo dog". What was a "banjo dog"? "Ah, my banjo dog!! Oh, oh! Oh, oh! Ah, my banjo dog!"'

I've been frustrated for years in my efforts to find out what a banjo dog is. I sometimes have the feeling that thousands of people must know, a kind of insider's knowledge; I just haven't run into anyone with that knowledge yet.

A bluegrass musician called Gene Parsons recorded an instrumental piece called 'Banjo Dog' back in the early Seventies. I asked him if he knew what a banjo dog was, and he told me he thought he'd invented the phrase and that it was meaningless. But I've made some other inquiries more recently, and think I may be able to solve the puzzle. It seems that a banjo dog is a fanciful fusion of the stereotypical hillbilly picking away at his banjo and the devoted bloodhound sitting by his rocker on the porch. On the internet, you can actually find sites featuring cartoons of the thing ...

Well, that's the most plausible explanation I've come across as yet, and I'm grateful to you – even if I'm not entirely convinced.

I mentioned Walker Evans a moment or two ago. 'Banjo Dog Variations' puts me in mind of another great photographer of the Thirties, Dorothea

Lange, mainly, I suppose, because of the poem's reference to the White Angel Breadline in San Francisco, which was the subject of one of her most famous photographs. You lived through the period, of course, and have memories of it to draw on, but did the photographs of Evans, Lange, Rothstein and the others played a part in the genesis of your poems about the Depression?

Absolutely, a big part. The O'Neal book I mentioned a moment ago gives a generous selection of the Farm Security Administration photographs, many made by the very photographers you speak of, as well as perhaps half a dozen others. The quatrain you've just quoted happens to come from a photograph made for the FSA by Marion Post Wolcott in Montana. The last stanza was prompted by a Lange photograph made in Oakland, California.

Reviewing the Library of America's American Poetry: The Twentieth Century, *Brad Leithauser recently wrote: 'The dust of steady motion is still in the air. But eventually, in a decade or two, it will surely be plain that in the last half of the twentieth century we were witnesses to an amazing era, one in which more good poets were writing than at any other time, before or since, in our nation's history.' Would you agree with that?*

I don't think I would. There have been more of us writing than ever before, certainly – a population explosion of poets – but the first three decades of the twentieth century were very strong and I think more than made up in quality for any lack in quantity. There were plenty of good American poets writing back then: Pound, Eliot, Stevens, Frost, Williams, Crane, perhaps, Auden (if we may count him amongst the Americans). And there are others, already half-forgotten. Of course, I may feel the power of these poets more strongly than a later generation would, since early, at a crucial time, they became a part of my own sensibility in ways no poets who came after could ever be. I saw the world through their eyes, heard it with their ears.

We spoke earlier about Harry Ford, your editor at Atheneum, and then at Knopf. His death in 1999 seems to have come as a huge blow to the many distinguished poets he'd worked with, as the tributes published in American Poet *attested. What made him such a good editor, would you say?*

Harry was a man with his own firm opinions on practically everything, and with great if not impeccable taste in poetry. He loved it and he loved working with us poets. Like a favourite uncle. But mainly, once he decided you were good, he let you go ahead and do whatever you wanted to do. He trusted you not to betray your talent. And when you came into town he gave you great lunches.

The latest issue of American Poet *contains a tribute by you and Robert Mezey to your old friend Edgar Bowers, who died in 2000. Now that metrical poetry is making a come-back – gone, thankfully, are the days when even quite intelligent people could say such things as that the use of accentual-syllabic metres was 'the principal way in which the educated classes of Europe mystified their utterance and gave it repressive authority, which they called poetry' – would you expect the audience for his work to grow?*

One could hope, but not too hopefully. Your view of the present situation seems too optimistic to me. And if I may say so, I think a critical passage like the one you quote is so baleful that it automatically disqualifies its author from being numbered among the quite intelligent people of the world.

In the last ten years or so, you've edited or co-edited a handful of volumes by poets dead before their time, amongst them The Collected Poems of Henri Coulette *(University of Arkansas Press, 1990), and Joe Bolton's* The Last Nostalgia: Poems 1982-1990 *(University of Arkansas Press, 1999). Could I ask you to say something about these two poets, who are virtually unheard of here.*

Coulette should certainly be held firmly in memory. His poetry is beautiful and elegant, with a mordant and exquisite wit, and his *The War of the Secret Agents* has to be one of the finest poems of any length in our time.

Is there a shorter poem of his you'd like to quote to demonstrate these qualities?

I could have chosen any one of a number – 'The Extras', 'Newfangleness', 'Petition', 'Cinema, at the Lighthouse' ... But I ended up choosing 'Night Thoughts':

NIGHT THOUGHTS
In memory of David Kubal

Your kind of night, David, your kind of night.
The dog would eye you as you closed your book;
Such a long chapter, such a time it took.
The great leaps! The high cries! The leash like a line drive!
The two of you would rove the perfumed street,
Pillar to post, and terribly alive.

Your kind of night, nothing more, nothing less;
A single lighted window, the shade drawn,
Your shadow enormous on the silver lawn,
The busy mockingbird, his rapturous fit,
The cricket keeping time, the loneliness
Of the man in the moon – and the man under it.

The word *elsewhere* was always on your lips,
A password to some secret, inner place
Where Wisdome smiled in Beautie's looking-glass
And Pleasure was at home to dearest Honour.
(The dog-eared pages mourn your fingertips,
And vehicle whispers, *Yet once more*, to tenor.)

Now you are elsewhere, *elsewhere* comes to this,
The thoughtless body, like a windblown rose,
Is gathered up and ushered toward repose.
To have to know this is our true condition,
The Horn of Nothing, the classical abyss,
The only cry a cry of recognition.

The priest wore purple; now the night does, too.
A dog barks, and another, and another.
There are a hundred words for the word *brother*.
We use them when we love, when we are sick,
And in our dreams when we are somehow you.
What are we if not wholly catholic?

And Joe Bolton, one of whose poems you quoted for us earlier? How would you describe him, for people who've not yet seen The Last Nostalgia?

Bolton was the youthful master of a fluent and casual-seeming metrical style. His poems are full of the sharply recorded social detail of his brief life and full to the brim of emotions that sometimes spill over most movingly.

You've said that his poems came to you as a result of his having told a friend, some time before his suicide, 'that if anything should ever happen to him ... I should get these poems to Donald Justice.' Had you had any prior contact with him, or had he simply recognized in you a kindred spirit?

He had been a student of mine at the University of Florida, one of the three or four most brilliant I ever had. And in regard to poetry, I do think we were kindred spirits.

Are there any other poets whose work you'd like a publisher to help us discover, or re-discover?

My old friend Robert Vaughn, for one.

Oh yes, you mentioned Vaughn earlier, and I promised to come back to him. He was another of the people to whose memory you dedicated The Sunset Maker, *a friend from your Miami years, and someone whose wayward life and violent death you've written about on a number of occasions. How good a poet was he, do you think? I ask because, while talking about the incomplete manuscript of his work you have in your possession – which I believe was gathered together after his death – you speak about fragments and stanzas, rather than whole poems, possessing great beauty, and of having to ransack the manuscript for passages to quote.*

My view of his poetry will always be coloured by my memory of him as a friend. He led too ragged and dangerous a life to settle down and concentrate on writing poems. In a way, the life he chose to live became his most fully realized art. His poems have beautifully intense and vivid flashes and patches, extremely romantic in spirit, but to me none of them seems to work all the way through. Well, that's true of most of the poems one reads, I guess. At some point that probably seems not to matter as much as one might think. And some of Vaughn's best poems are surely lost. All in all, there are just not enough poems to make up a book, and for years I have vainly urged my printer friends to undertake a chapbook of his work, which would be slender but very worthwhile. So far, no takers.

You said that Vaughn was just one of the poets whose work you'd like to see in print, or back in print. Who else?

Ronald Perry would be another ...

Another friend from your Miami years ...

He published one slim book of poems and a couple of chapbooks in the Fifties and Sixties, and then gave up writing for the best part of twenty years ...

Only to be got going again when you proposed that he be featured in Random House's National Poetry Series.

Yes, and once that volume, *Denizens,* was settled on, he began to write furiously again and soon had enough new poems for another book, which he was given to believe Random House would publish. Then, quite suddenly, Ronald dropped dead – and his death wiped out any interest the publisher had in the book. Nearly twenty years later the manuscript survives, though barely, in a box in my chaotic studio, and I think there's probably another copy more easily to be turned up in Dana Gioia's study-house in California.

In the late 1980s, Stephen Parrish, the general editor of the Cornell Wordsworth, *published an article in which he attacked something he called 'the whig interpretation of literature', this being the habit – widespread among editors, so he claimed – of assuming that a text's evolution is synonymous with its improvement. I doubt that any serious editor ever made such an assumption, but let's leave that on one side. Parrish so disapproved of it, that he thought the best policy was simply to turn it on its head. Thus in the foreword to the* Cornell Wordsworth, *he wrote: 'Wordsworth's practice of leaving his poems unpublished for years after their completion and his lifelong habit of revision … have obscured the original, often thought the best, versions of his work. These original versions are here presented in the form of clean, continuous "reading texts" from which all layers of later revision have been stripped away. In volumes that cover the work of Wordsworth's middle and later years, bringing the "early Wordsworth" into view means simply presenting as "reading texts", wherever possible, the earliest finished versions of the poems, not the latest revised versions.' We've already seen how devoted you are to what you've called 'wholesale revision, and large swooping cuts', and what I'd like to ask is how you feel about the earlier versions of your poems once their respective boxes have clicked shut? Would the prospect of a Cornell Justice, edited by a latterday Parrish, appeal to, or appal, you?*

I'm sorry but I don't know Parrish's version of Wordsworth. The prospect appals more than it appeals. His practice would deprive the poet of his second thought. It seems by implication to endorse, perhaps unconsciously, an ancient and rather naïve idea of inspiration. It's true that after revising a poem I sometimes will go back to the original version. But the first version is hardly sacrosanct. One looks for the best version whenever that stage may be reached, and the author is the only one who has the right to decide that, really. What might be fascinating and instructive is an edition which printed first and final versions on facing pages. Surely this must have been done, though I can't call up an example.

Can I ask what you're working on now – or what you'll go back to working on once you're through with answering all of these questions, at any rate?

Not much. A blank verse narrative – a monologue, really – set in Miami

Beach at the end of WWII, but on this one I may be hopelessly stuck. Also trying a little music – a piece for cello and piano, for instance, based on the musical phrase quoted in 'The Sunset Maker'.

Are there any plans for a Collected Poems?

No plans, but if I live long enough I'd like to collect everything – well, not quite everything. I could probably use Harry Ford's advice on this.

At the Young Composers' Concert

Sewanee, Tennessee, summer, 1996

The melancholy of these young composers
Impresses me. There will be time for joy.

Meanwhile, one can't help noticing the boy
Who bends down to his violin as if

To comfort it in its too early grief.
It is his composition, confused and sad,

Made out of feelings he has not yet had
But only caught somehow the rumour of

In the old scores – and that has been enough.
Merely mechanical, sure, all artifice –

But can that matter when it sounds like this?
What matters is the beauty of the attempt,

The world for him being so far mostly dreamt.
Not that a lot, to tell the truth, has passed,

Nothing to change our lives or that will last.
And not that we are awed exactly; still,

There is something to this beyond mere adult skill.
And if it moves but haltingly down its scales,

It is the more moving just because it fails;
And is the lovelier because we know

It has gone beyond itself, as great things go.

Ralph:
A Love Story

In what had been a failing music store
A man named Flowers opened the first cinema
In Moultrie. Ralph was the projectionist,
At seventeen the first projectionist.
And there was an old upright from the store
On which the wife accompanied the action
With little bursts of von Suppé and Wagner.

Ralph liked the dark of the projection booth;
He liked the flickering images of the screen.
And yet because he liked it all so well,
He feared expulsion from this little Eden,
Not so much feared as knew the day must come,
Given his luck, when it would all run out,
Which made the days more paradisal still.

Margot, the daughter, twenty and unmarried –
To tell it all quickly – seduced Ralph.
She let him think he was seducing her.
They used to meet in the projection booth,
Embracing wordlessly but laughing too,
Unable to suppress their self-delight.
Time after time they had almost been caught.
Then, as in novels, Margot became pregnant.

Sundays the cinema was closed.
                              Ralph packed
And slipped off to the depot about dusk.
That night from the train he watched with a kind of nostalgia
The sparse pale farmlights passing from his life –
And he understood nothing, only that he was young.
Within a week or two he joined the navy.

Not that he realized it at the time,
But those quick laughing grapplings in the dark
Would be the great romance his life would know
Though there would be more women, more than he wanted
Really, before it was all finished for him.
And even in the last few years, working
His final job, night watchman at a warehouse,

He would be resting on a stack of lumber
Toward morning, say, and there would come to him
The faces of the stars before the stars
Had names, only dark-painted eyes, and hands
That spoke the sign-language of the secret heart.
(Oh, not that he remembered. He did not.)

She wrote him over the first months two letters
In care of his parents in another town.
The envelopes were boldly decorated
With home-drawn hearts, some broken, pierced by arrows.
And the mother must have guessed the truth and thought
To spare the son by keeping back the letters

Until the time seemed ripe for him to have them.
And when his tour of duty finally ended
He did unseal and read them and was sorry.
It had been the happiness of his life.
But he could not go back to it. He could not.

So it was gone, the way a thing will go
Yet keep a sort of phantom presence always.
He might be drinking with some woman, lying
Beside her on a tourist cabin bed,
When something would come ghosting back to him,
Some little thing. Such paradise it had been!

And when it *was* all finished for him, at the end,
In the small bedroom of his sister's house,
Surrounded by his shelves of paperbacks –
Westerns mostly, and a few private-eyes –
Lying there on the single bed, half gone
On Echo Springs, he could not call it back.
Or if it came back it was in the form
Of images in the dark, shifting and flashing,
Badly projected, spooling out crazily
In darkness, in a little room, and he
Could not control it. It was like dying.
No, it *was* dying, and he let it go.

THE THIRTIES: PAY DAY

THE THIRTIES: PAYDAY

Donald Justice

THE THIRTIES: STREET BAND   Donald Justice

THE THIRTIES: CAFÉ   Donald Justice

RAINY EVENING: VENICE

Sherwood Anderson

Winesburg
Nine short pieces for tenor and string trio

Donald Justice

FROM

Night Piece (Nocturne)
For Piano

3. NIGHT PIECE (NOCTURNE)

BIBLIOGRAPHY

COMPILED BY DANNY GILLANE

WITH THE ASSISTANCE OF DONALD JUSTICE AND PHILIP HOY

This bibliography is extracted from *The Donald Justice Bibliography*, a full descriptive work which will be published in the near future by Parrish House of Jackson, Mississippi.

PRIMARY WORKS

POETRY

BOOKS

The Old Bachelor and Other Poems. Miami, Florida: Pandanus Press, 1951.

The Summer Anniversaries. Middletown, Connecticut: Wesleyan University Press, 1960.

A Local Storm. Iowa City, Iowa: Stone Wall Press and The Finial Press, 1963.

Three Poems. With drypoints by Virginia Piersol. Iowa City, Iowa: University of Iowa, 1966.

Night Light. Middletown, Connecticut: Wesleyan University Press, 1967.

Four Poets: Tom McAfee, Donald Drummond, Donald Justice, R.P. Dickey. Ed. Charles L. Willig. Pella, Iowa: Central College, 1967.

Sixteen Poems. Iowa City, Iowa: Stone Wall Press, 1970.

From a Notebook. Iowa City, Iowa: Seamark Press, 1972.

L'Homme qui se ferme: A Poem by Guillevic/The Man Closing Up: A Translation and an Improvisation by Donald Justice. Iowa City, Iowa: Stone Wall Press, 1973.

Departures. Iowa City, Iowa: Penumbra Press/Stone Wall Press, 1973.

Departures. New York: Atheneum, 1973.

Selected Poems. New York: Atheneum, 1979.

Selected Poems. London: Anvil Press Poetry, 1980.

The Summer Anniversaries. Revised edition. Middletown, Connecticut: Wesleyan University Press, 1981.

Night Light. Revised edition. Middletown, Connecticut: Wesleyan University Press, 1981.

Tremayne: Four Poems by Donald Justice. Iowa City, Iowa: Windhover Press, 1984.

Platonic Scripts. Ann Arbor, Michigan: University of Michigan Press, 1984.

The Sunset Maker: Poems/Stories/A Memoir. New York: Atheneum, 1987.

The Sunset Maker: Poems/Stories/A Memoir. London: Anvil Press Poetry, 1987.

The Death of Lincoln /A Documentary Opera by Edwin London /On an Original Libretto by Donald Justice. Austin, Texas: W. Thomas Taylor, 1988.

A Donald Justice Reader. Hanover, New Hampshire: University Press of New England, 1991.

Banjo Dog: Poems and Linocut Illustrations by Donald Justice. Riverside, California: Thaumatrope Press, 1995.

New and Selected Poems. New York: Knopf, 1995.

Oblivion: On Writers and Writing. Ashland, Oregon: Story Line Press, 1998.

Orpheus Hesitated Beside the Black River: Poems, 1952-1997. London: Anvil Press Poetry, 1998.

Ralph: A Love Story. West Chester, Philadelphia: Aralia Press, 1999.

BROADSIDES AND EPHEMERA

Spring Poetry Festival at Wesleyan: Four Poets: Philip Booth, Donald Justice, Paul Ramsey, James Wright. Middleton, Connecticut: Wesleyan University, 1960.
In the Attic. West Branch, Iowa: The Toothpaste Press, 1980.
Men at Forty. Colorado Springs, Colorado: The Press at Colorado College, 1985.
Young Girls Growing Up (1911). Minneapolis, Minnesota: Minnesota Centre for the Book Arts, 1988.
[On a Woman of Spirit Who Taught Both Piano and Dance]. New York: Knopf, 1995. Postcard.
A Certain Oriental on His Deathbed. West Chester, Philadelphia: Aralia Press, 1996.
The Ballad of Charles Starkweather. With Robert Mezey. West Chester, Philadelphia: Aralia Press, 1997. See under INDIVIDUAL POEMS for an earlier version of this poem.
There is a gold light in certain old paintings. New York: Academy of American Poets, 1998.

INDIVIDUAL POEMS

BH = *BEYOND THE HUNTING WOODS AND OTHER POEMS* (1954)
DE = *DEPARTURES* (1973)
DJ = *A DONALD JUSTICE READER* (1991)
LS = *A LOCAL STORM* (1963)
NL = *NIGHT LIGHT* (1967)
NS= *NEW AND SELECTED POEMS* (1995)
OB = *THE OLD BACHELOR AND OTHER POEMS* (1951)
OH = *ORPHEUS HESITATED BESIDE THE BLACK RIVER* (1998)
SA = *THE SUMMER ANNIVERSARIES* (1960)
SP = *SELECTED POEMS* (1979)
SM = *THE SUNSET MAKER* (1987)
SP = *SIXTEEN POEMS* (1979)
TP = *THREE POEMS* (1966)

'A Broken Engagement'. *Factotum*, 1 (May 1948): 30.
'A Certain Oriental on His Deathbed'. OB: 6.
'A Dancer's Life'. DE: 6-7; SP: 77.
'A Dream Sestina'. NS: 35-36; DJ: 44-45. Published elsewhere as 'Sestina: A Dream'.
'A Farm Near Tifton, Georgia, c. 1930'. Published elsewhere as 'The Silent World' and as part 1 of 'Memories of the Depression Years'.
'A Letter'. DE: 5; SP:90; NS: 98.
'A Local Storm'. LS; NL: 24; NS: 69
'A Man of 1794'. NS: 14; OH: 106-107.
'A Map of Love'. NS: 47. Published elsewhere as 'Love's Map'.
'A Variation on Baudelaire's "La Servante au Grand Coeur"'. NS: 7-8; OH: 99-100.
'A Winter Ode to the Old Men of Lummus Park, Miami, Florida'. SA: 45; DJ: 25; NS: 50; OH: 24.
'ABC'. DE: 3.
'Aboard! Aboard!'. BH: 15.
'Absences'. DE: 51. SP: 102; DJ: 29; NS: 115; OH: 58.
'After a Phrase Abandoned by Wallace Stevens'. NL: 30-31. A shortened version of this poem was published in SP: 38 and DJ: 90.

'After School Practice: A Short Story'. DJ: 109. Published elsewhere as 'After School Practice: An Episode'.

'After School Practice: An Episode'. SM: 48. Published elsewhere as 'After School Practice: A Short Story'.

'After the Chinese'. DE: 27.

'American Scenes (1904-1905)'. Comprising 'Cambridge in Winter', 'Railway Junction South of Richmond, Past Midnight', St Michael's Cemetery, Charleston', 'Epilogue: Coronado Beach, California'. NS: 141-142; OH: 76-77.

'American Sketches'. Comprising 'Crossing Kansas by Train' and 'Poem to Be Read at 3 A.M.'. NL: 28-29; SP: 47-48; NS: 72-73.

'An American in Venice (Holy Saturday)'. *Factotum*, I (May 1948): 28-29.

'An Elegy Is Preparing Itself'. DE: 35; SP: 97.

'An Old-Fashioned Devil'. NS: 119. Published elsewhere as part 2 of 'On the Devil in Our Time', and as 'Sonnet: An Old-Fashioned Devil'.

'Angel Death Blues'. See 'Two Blues'.

'Anniversaries'. SA: 3-4. Published elsewhere, in substantially altered form, as 'The Summer Anniversaries'.

'Anonymous Drawing'. NL: 26; SP: 33; NS: 71; OH: 36.

'Another Song'. SA: 40; SP: 8; DJ: 80; NS: 71; OH: 36.

'Anthony Street'. Comprising 'Morning. The roofs emerge, the yard – ', 'Evening. The paper-boy on wheels'. SP: 22. Published elsewhere as 'Anthony St. Blues'.

'Anthony St. Blues'. Comprising 'Morning. The roofs emerge, the yard – ', 'Evening. The paper-boy on wheels'. SA: 44. Published elsewhere as 'Anthony Street'.

'At a Rehearsal of "Uncle Vanya"'. NL: 61-62. Published elsewhere as 'At a Rehearsal of *Uncle Vanya*.

'At a Rehearsal of *Uncle Vanya*'. SP: 52; DJ: 71-72; NS: 91. Published elsewhere as 'At a Rehearsal of "Uncle Vanya"'.

'At the Cemetery'. See 'My South'.

'At the Young Composers' Concert: Sewanee, Tennessee, Summer, 1996'. *Oxford American*, 34 (July-August 2000): 45.

'Bad Dreams'. An unfinished poem, comprising 'Chorus', 'Speaker', 'Epilogue: To the Morning Light'. NS: 55-59. A shorter version, comprising 'Speaker' and 'Epilogue : To the Morning Light' published in DJ: 29-30.

'Banjo Dog Variations'. BD; NS: 19-21.

'Beyond the Hunting Woods'. BH: 29-30; SA: 22-23; SP: 15.

'Body and Soul'. Comprising 'Hotel', 'Rain' and 'Street Musician'. NS: 15-16; DJ: 38-39; OH: 108-109.

'Boston, Georgia, c. 1933'. See 'Memories of the Depression Years'.

'Bus Stop'. NL: 57; SP: 50; DJ: 78; NS: 86; OH: 43.

'Busted Dreams: Mrs L'. See 'The Piano Teachers: A Memoir of the Thirties'.

'But That Is Another Story'. NL: 20; SP: 35; NS: 67.

'Cambridge in Winter'. See 'American Scenes (1904-1905)'.

'Cemetery'. See 'My South'.

'Cemetery in the Snow'. Translation of 'Cementerio en la nieve' by Xavier Villaurrutia. Ed. Mark Strand. *New Poetry of Mexico*. New York: E.P. Dutton, 1970: 159.

'Childhood'. NS: 131-133; DJ: 26-28; NS: 131-133; OH: 68-70.

'Children Walking Home from School through Good Neighbourhood'. SM: 11; DJ: 18; NS: 145; OH: 79.

'Chorus'. DJ: 15. See 'Bad Dreams'.

'Cinema and Ballad of the Great Depression'. SM: 23-24; DJ: 23-24; NS: 158-159.

'Clock'. See 'Things'.

'Cool Dark Ode'. See 'Three Odes'.

'Counting the Mad'. BH: 20; SA: 46; SP: 14; DJ: 77; NS: 51; OH: 25.

'Couplets Concerning Time'. OH: 122.

'Crossing Kansas by Train'. DJ: 3. Published elsewhere as part 1 of 'American Sketches'.

'Dance Lessons of the Thirties'. DJ: 108; OH: 111.

'Don Juan's Song'. See 'Two Songs from "Don Juan in Hell"'.

'Dreams of Water'. NL: 17-18; SP: 44-45; DJ: 96-97.

'Early Poems'. NL: 36; SP: 46; NS: 77.

'Elsewheres'. Comprising 'South', 'North', and 'Waiting Room'. NL: 32-34; SP: 63-64; NS: 74-75.

'Epilogue: Coronado Beach, California'. See 'American Scenes (1904-1905)'.

'Epilogue: To the Morning Light'. DJ: 16-17; NS: 58-59; OH: 30-31. See 'Bad Dreams'.

'Epitaph for a Pair of Old Shoes'. New Republic, 221:7 (August 1999): 38.

'Epitaph in the Form of a Bookplate for a Volume of the Romantic Poets'. OB: 10.

'Farm'. See 'My South'.

'First Death'. Comprising 'June 12, 1933', 'June 13, 1933', and 'June 14, 1933'. SP: 119-121; DJ: 12-14; NS: 122-124; OH: 59-61.

'Five Portraits'. Comprising 'Portrait with Short Hair', 'Portrait with Flashlight', 'Portrait with Tequila', 'Portrait with One Eye', and 'Self-Portrait as Still Life'. DE: 8-12. Published elsewhere as 'Portraits of the Sixties'.

'For a Freshman Reader'. NL: 67-68.

'For the Suicides'. NS: 82-83. Published elsewhere as 'For the Suicides of 1962' and 'The Suicides'.

'For the Suicides of 1962'. NL: 52-54; OH: 38-40. Published elsewhere as 'For the Suicides' and 'The Suicides'.

'Fragment: To a Mirror'. DE: 4; SP 73; DJ: 70; NS: 97.

'From a Notebook'. DE: 28-29; SP: 98-100; NS: 103-104.

'Girl Sitting Alone at Party'. NL: 22.

'Hands'. NL: 47; SP: 68.

'Heart'. NL: 21; SP: 29; DJ: 93; NS: 68.

'Hell'. DJ: 54; NS: 154; OH: 86. Published elsewhere as 'Purgatory'.

'Henry James by the Pacific'. DJ: 5. Published elsewhere as 'Epilogue: Coronado Beach, California'.

'Here in Katmandu'. SA: 16-17; DJ: 48-49; NS: 39-40; OH: 18-19. Published elsewhere as 'Sestina: Here in Katmandu'.

'High Place'. Translation of 'Haut Lieu' by André Pieyre de Mandiargues. Eds. Alexander Aspel and Donald Justice. Contemporary French Poetry: Fourteen Witnesses of Man's Fate. Ann Arbor, Michigan: University of Michigan Press, 1965: 105.

'Homage to the Memory of Wallace Stevens'. DE: 40-41; SP:88-89; DJ: 88-89; NS: 107-108.

'Homecoming'. BH: 16.

'Hotel'. See 'Body and Soul'.

'Houses'. NL: 13. Published elsewhere, and in a slightly different form, as 'Time and the Weather' and 'Time and the Weather Wear Away'.

'Humbly'. Translation of 'Humildemente' by R. López Velarde. Ed. Mark Strand, New Poetry of Mexico. New York: E.P. Dutton, 1970: 195.

'In Bertram's Garden'. BH: 10; SA: 41; SP:7; DJ: 92; NS: 49; OH: 23.

'In Memory of Mrs. Snow, My First Piano Teacher'. The Atlantic 258: 5 (November 1986): 122.

'In Memory of My Friend the Bassoonist John Lenox'. SM: 16-17; NS: 151-152.

'In Memory of the Unknown Poet, Robert Boardman Vaughn'. SM: 18; DJ: 53; NS: 153;

OH: 85.

'In the Attic'. SP: 130; DJ: 35; NS: 129; OH:66.

'In the Cemetery'. *The Atlantic* 250:3 (September 1982): 76.

'In the Greenroom'. NL: 60; SP: 51; DJ: 73; NS: 90.

'Incident in a Rose Garden'. ['Gardener: Sir I encountered Death']. NL: 58-59; DJ: 66-67; OH: 44-45. Published elsewhere as 'Incident in a Rose Garden (1)'.

'Incident in a Rose Garden'. ['The gardener came running']. SP: 65-66. Published elsewhere as 'Incident in a Rose Garden (2)'.

'Incident in a Rose Garden (1)'. NS: 87. Published elsewhere as one of two poems entitled 'Incident in a Rose Garden'.

'Incident in a Rose Garden (2)'. NS: 88-89. Published elsewhere as one of two poems entitled 'Incident in a Rose Garden'.

'Invitation to a Ghost'. NS: 9; OH: 101.

'It Was a Kind and Northern Face: Mrs. Snow'. See 'The Piano Teachers: A Memoir of the Thirties'.

'June 12, 1933'. See 'First Death'.

'June 13, 1933'. See 'First Death'.

'June 14, 1933'. See 'First Death'.

'Kiting'. *Literary Review* (Summer 1962).

'La jeune fille à l'imperméable noir'. With Dori Katz. Ed. George Garrett. *The Girl in the Black Raincoat*. New York: Duell, Sloan and Pearce, 1966. See 'The Girl in the Black Raincoat'.

'Ladies by Their Windows'. BH: 11-13; SA: 32-34; SP: 3-4; NS: 44-46.

'Landscape with Little Figures'. SA: 9; SP: 6; DJ: 91; NS: 32; OH: 13.

'Last Days of Prospero'. NL: 63-64; SP: 36-37; DJ: 74-75; NS: 92-93; OH: 46-47.

'Last Evening'. SM: 14. Published elsewhere as 'Last Evening: At the Piano'.

'Last Evening: At the Piano'. DJ: 84; NS: 148; OH: 82. Published elsewhere as 'Last Evening'.

'Lesbians'. BH: 8.

'Lethargy'. DE: 13; NS: 101. See 'Two Small Vices Beginning with the Letter "L"'.

'Lightning Victory'. Translation of 'Victoire éclair' by René Char. With Dori Katz. Eds. Alexander Aspel and Donald Justice. *Contemporary French Poetry: Fourteen Witnesses of Man's Fate*. Ann Arbor, Michigan: University of Michigan Press, 1965: 67.

'Lines at the New Year'. SM: 3.

'Little Elegy'. SP: 118; DJ: 82; NS: 121.

'Little Elegy for Cello and Piano'. DJ: 127-131.

'Lorca in California'. NS: 5-6.

'Lorcaesques'. DE: 26.

'Love's Map'. SA: 37. Published elsewhere as 'A Map of Love'.

'Love's Stratagems'. SA: 36.

'Luxury'. DE: 14. See 'Two Small Vices Beginning with the Letter "L"'.

'Manhattan Dawn (1945)'. SM 25; DJ: 37.

'Memo from the Desk of X'. *Night Light*: 65-66.

'Memories of Iza'. Translation of 'Recuerdos de Iza' by Carlos Pellicer. Ed. Mark Strand. *New Poetry of Mexico*. New York: E.P. Dutton, 1970: 171.

'Memories of the Depression Years'. Comprising 'A Farm Near Tifton, Georgia, C. 1930', 'Boston, Georgia, C. 1933', 'Miami, Florida, C. 1936'. SP 128-129; DJ: 21-22; NS: 127-128; OH: 64-65.

'Memory of a Porch'. NL: 19; SP: 49.

'Men at Forty'. NL: 35; DJ: 94; NS: 76; OH: 37.

'Miami, Florida'. See 'Memories of the Depression Years'.

'Mirror'. See 'Things'.

'Monologue in an Attic'. DJ: 33.

'Mrs Snow'. SM: 32; DJ: 105; NS: 165; OH: 93.

'Mule Team and Poster'. SM: 4; NS: 137; OH: 71.

'My South'. The first version of this, comprising 'Cemetery', 'Farm' and 'Train', was published in SM: 5-6; a later version, comprising 'On the Porch', 'At the Cemetery', 'On the Farm', 'On the Train, Heading North Through Florida, Late at Night and Long Ago, and Ending with a Line from Thomas Wolfe', was published in NS: 138-140 and in OH: 72-75.

'Narcissus at Home'. NL: 75-77.

'Nineteenth-Century Portrait'. SM: 9; NS: 143; OH: 78.

'1971'. DE: 25.

'1980—December 12'. Seneca Review 21:2 (1991): 95.

'Nocturne of the Statue'. Translation of 'Nocturno de la estatua' by Xavier Villaurrutia. Ed. Mark Strand. New Poetry of Mexico. New York: E.P. Dutton, 1970: 149.

'North'. See 'Elsewheres'.

'Nostalgia and Complaint of the Grandparents'. SM: 21-22; NS: 156-157.

'Nostalgia of the Lakefronts'. SM: 26-27; DJ: 30-31; NS: 160-161; OH: 88-89.

'October: A Song'. SM: 12; DJ: 79; NS: 146; OH: 80.

'Ode to a Dressmaker's Dummy'. NL: 18; SP: 31; DJ: 34; NS: 66; OH: 34.

'Old Man to a Young Woman'. OB: 8.

'On a Painting by Patient B of the Independence State Hospital for the Insane'. BH: 21-22; SA: 47-48; SP: 13; DJ: 76; NS: 52; OH: 26-27.

'On a Picture by Burchfield'. NS: 3.

'On a Snapshot of My Grandfather'. BH: 18.

'On a Woman of Spirit Who Taught Both Piano and Dance'. DJ: 107; OH: 110.

'On an Anniversary'. NS: 13; OH: 105.

'On the Blank Card'. December 1:2 (May 1958): 12.

'On the Death of Friends in Childhood'. SA: 10; SP: 23; DJ: 61; NS: 33; OH: 14.

'On the Devil in Our Time'. Comprising 'A dwarfish, pious, country kind of fool', 'Who is it snarls our plough-lines, wastes our fields'. OB: 4-5. The first of the two poems was published elsewhere as 'Sonnet: An Old-Fashioned Devil'.

'On the Farm'. See 'My South'.

'On the Night of the Departure by Bus'. DE: 17.

'On the Porch'. See 'My South'.

'On the Train, Heading North Through Florida, Late at Night and Long Ago, and Ending with a Line from Thomas Wolfe'. See 'My South'.

'Ophelia'. BH: 7.

'Order in the Streets'. Ed. Meyer, Michael. The Bedford Introduction to Literature, 2nd ed. Boston: Bedford Books of St. Martin Press, 1990: 673-674.

'Orpheus Opens His Morning Mail'. NL: 9; SP: 41; OH: 32.

'Pale Tepid Ode'. See 'Three Odes'.

'Pantoum of the Depression Years'. NS: 22-23; OH: 116-117.

'Party'. NL: 23.

'Pillow'. See 'Things'.

'Poem'. DE: 38-39; SP: 82; DJ: 99; NS: 106; OH: 56.

'Poem for a Survivor'. NL: 71.

'Poem to be Read at 3 A.M'. DJ: 4. One of two poems published elsewhere under the group title 'American Sketches'.

'Portrait with Flashlight'. DJ: 56. See 'Five Portraits' and 'Portraits of the Sixties'.

'Portrait with One Eye'. DJ: 55; NS: 99. See 'Five Portraits' and 'Portraits of the Sixties'.
'Portrait with Short Hair'. See 'Five Portraits' and 'Portraits of the Sixties'.
'Portrait with Tequila'. See 'Five Portraits' and 'Portraits of the Sixties'.
'Portraits of the Sixties'. Comprising 'Portrait with Short Hair', 'Portrait with Flashlight', 'Portrait with Tequila', 'Portrait with One Eye', and 'Self-Portrait as Still Life'. OH: 48-52. Published elsewhere as 'Five Portraits'.
'Prayer'. *Accent* 14:4 (Autumn 1954): 271. Published elsewhere as 'To Satan in Heaven'.
'Presences'. DE: 52; SP: 103.
'Prodigal Poem'. Translation of 'Poema pródigo' by Carlos Pellicer. Ed. Mark Strand. *New Poetry of Mexico*. New York: E.P. Dutton, 1970: 177.
'Psalm and Lament'. SM: 15; DJ: 62; NS: 149.
'Purgatory'. SM: 19. Published elsewhere as 'Hell'.
'Railway Junction South of Richmond, Past Midnight'. See 'American Scenes (1904-1905)'.
'Rain'. See 'Body and Soul'.
'Ralph: A Love Story'. *Ralph: A Love Story*. West Chester, Philadelphia: Aralia Press, 1999; *New Criterion* 17:10 (June 1999): 34.
'Riddle'. DE: 30; SP: 108.
'Rose Nocturnal'. Translation of 'Nocturna Rosa' by Xavier Villaurrutia. Ed. Mark Strand. *New Poetry of Mexico*. New York: E.P. Dutton, 1970: 155.
'Rule'. Translation of 'Regle' by Francis Ponge. Eds. Alexander Aspel and Donald Justice. *Contemporary French Poetry: Fourteen Witnesses of Man's Fate*. Ann Arbor, Michigan: University of Michigan Press: 1965: 29.
'Sadness'. NS: 24-25; OH: 118.
'Seawind: A Song'. SM: 13. Published elsewhere as 'Sea-Wind: A Song' and 'Sea Wind: A Song'.
'Sea-Wind: A Song'. DJ: 83. Published elsewhere as 'Seawind: A Song' and 'Sea Wind: A Song'.
'Sea Wind: A Song'. NS: 147; OH: 81. Published elsewhere as 'Seawind: A Song' and Sea-Wind: A Song.
'Self-Portrait as Still Life'. NS: 100. See 'Five Portraits' and 'Portraits of the Sixties'.
'Sestina on Six Words by Weldon Kees'. SA: 14-15; DJ: 46-47; NS: 37-38; OH: 16-17.
'Sestina: A Dream'. SP: 18-19. Published elsewhere as 'A Dream Sestina'.
'Sestina: Here in Katmandu'. SP: 20-21. Published elsewhere as 'Here in Katmandu'.
'Sganarelle's Song'. See 'Two Songs from "Don Juan in Hell"'.
'Sonatina in Green'. DE: 42-43; SP: 104-105; DJ: 57-58.
'Sonatina in Yellow'. DE: 44-45; SP: 106-107; DJ: 59-60; NS: 109-110.
'Song' ['First was not']. *Accent*: 14:4 (Autumn 1954): 270.
'Song' ['Morning Opened']. SA: 5.
'Song: "Here Lies Love"'. OB: 7.
'Song of the Hours'. *Seneca Review* 21:2 (1991): 93-94.
'Song of the Nymph Bathing'. *Western Review* 17:1 (Autumn 1952): 25.
'Song of the State Troopers'. *Seneca Review* 21:2 (1991): 93.
'Songs'. BH: 31.
'Songs from *Don Juan in Hell*'. *Antaeus*, 20 (Winter 1976): 114-115. Published elsewhere as 'Two Songs from *Don Juan in Hell*'.
'Songs from the Telephone Booth in the Woods'. *Antaeus*, 20 (Winter 1976): 112-113.
'Sonnet'. BH: 24; Published elsewhere as 'Sonnet: The Wall' and 'The Wall'.
'Sonnet'. Translation of an untitled poem by Phillippe Jaccottet. Eds. Alexander Aspel and Donald Justice. *Contemporary French Poetry: Fourteen Witnesses of Man's Fate*.

Ann Arbor, Michigan: University of Michigan Press: 1965: 132.

'Sonnet about P'. SA: 39.

'Sonnet to My Father'. SA: 21; DJ: 7; NS: 41.

'Sonnet: An Old-Fashioned Devil'. SP: 111. Poem one of two published elsewhere under the group title 'On the Devil In Our Time'.

'Sonnet: The Wall'. SA: 11; SP: 10; Published elsewhere as 'Sonnet' and 'The Wall'.

'Sonnet: The Poet at Seven'. SP: 9.

'South'. See 'Elsewheres'.

'Southern Gothic'. SA: 20.

'Speaker'. See 'Bad Dreams'.

'Speaking of Islands'. SA: 38.

'St Michael's Cemetery, Charleston'. See 'American Scenes (1904-1905)'.

'Stone'. See 'Things'.

'Street Musician'. See 'Body and Soul'.

'Study'. Translation of 'Estudio' by Carlos Pellicer. Ed. Mark Strand. New Poetry of Mexico. New York: E.P. Dutton, 1970: 169.

'Studies'. Translation of 'Estidios' by Carlos Pellicer. Ed. Mark Strand. New Poetry of Mexico. New York: E.P. Dutton, 1970: 175.

'Sunday Afternoon in Buffalo, Texas'. SP. 127.

'Tales from a Family Album'. SA: 24-25; SP: 16; NS: 42.

'The Artist Orpheus'. NS: 4; OH: 98.

'The Assassination'. DE: 22; SP: 80.

'The Ballad of Charles Starkweather'. With Robert Mezey. Antaeus, 20 (Winter 1976): 110; a later version of this poem was published as The Ballad of Charles Starkweather. West Chester, Philadelphia: Aralia Press, 1997.

'The Bat'. BH: 27.

'The Colour of Cold'. Translation of 'La couleur du froid' by André Pieyre de Mandiargues. Eds. Alexander Aspel and Donald Justice. Contemporary French Poetry: Fourteen Witnesses of Man's Fate. Ann Arbor, Michigan: University of Michigan Press, 1965: 101.

'The Confession'. DE: 20; SP: 78.

'The Conspirators Make Their Vows' (Act I, Scene 3 of the libretto for Edwin London's opera). Michigan Quarterly Review 27:4 (Fall 1988): 586-593.

'The Contentment of Tremayne'. See 'Tremayne'.

'The Crossing'. Translation of 'La Traversée' by Phillippe Jaccottet. Eds. Alexander Aspel and Donald Justice. Contemporary French Poetry: Fourteen Witnesses of Man's Fate. Ann Arbor, Michigan: University of Michigan Press, 1965: 137.

'The Devil Disguised'. BH: 1.

'The Dream of the Black Gloves'. Translation of 'El sueño de los guantes negros' by R. López Velarde. Ed. Mark Strand. New Poetry of Mexico. New York: E.P. Dutton, 1970: 201.

'The Evening of the Mind'. NL: 51; SP: 43.

'The Exercise', With Susana Heringman. Translation of Fernando Arbelaez. Iowa Review 7:2-3 (Spring/Summer 1976): 81.

'The Furies'. SP: 117.

'The Girl in the Black Raincoat'. With Mark Strand. Ed. George Garrett. The Girl in the Black Raincoat. New York: Duell, Sloan and Pearce, 1966. See 'La jeune fille à l'imperméable noir'.

'The Grandfathers'. NL: 15; SP: 32; NS: 65.

'The Great American Poem'. *Antaeus,* 32 (Winter 1979): 82-86. A chain poem, only the first line of which is by DJ.

'The Insomnia of Tremayne'. See 'Tremayne'.

'The Library Is On Fire'. Translation of 'La bibliothèque est en feu' by René Char. With Ralph Freedman and Paulène Aspel. Eds. Alexander Aspel and Donald Justice. *Contemporary French Poetry: Fourteen Witnesses of Man's Fate.* Ann Arbor, Michigan: University of Michigan Press, 1965: 69-77.

'The Man Closing Up: Improvisations on Themes from Guillevic'. TP: [11-14]; NL: 42-46; *L'Homme qui se ferme: A Poem by Guillevic/The Man Closing Up: A Translation and an Improvisation by Donald Justice*; SP: 57-59; NS: 79-81.

'The Match'. Translation of 'L'Allumette' by Francis Ponge. With Dori Katz. Eds. Alexander Aspel and Donald Justice. *Contemporary French Poetry: Fourteen Witnesses of Man's Fate.* Ann Arbor, Michigan: University of Michigan Press, 1965: 31.

'The Metamorphoses of a Vampire'. DJ: 85.

'The Metamorphosis'. SA: 18-19.

'The Miami of Other Days'. NS: 11-12; OH: 103-104.

'The Mild Despair of Tremayne'. See 'Tremayne'.

'The Missing Person'. TP: [5-6]; NL: 40-41; SP: 61-62.

'The Old Bachelor'. OB:1-2.

'The Old Bachelor Buries His Sister'. BH: 3.

'The Old Bachelor Makes His Will'. BH: 4.

'The Piano Teachers: A Memoir of the Thirties'. Comprising 'It Was a Kind and Northern Face: Mrs Snow', 'Busted Dreams: Mrs L', 'Those Tropic Afternoons: Mrs K', SM: 43-46; DJ: 100-104; NS: 167-170.

'The Poet at Seven'. SA: 7; NS: 31. Published elsewhere as 'Sonnet: The Poet at Seven'.

'The Pupil'. SM: 47; DJ: 106; NS: 166; OH: 94.

'The Return of Alcestis'. SP: 112; NS: 120.

'The Scarred Men, She'. *Mademoiselle* (February 1943): 180.

'The Silent World'. *New England Review* 1:2 (Winter 1978): 132. Published elsewhere as 'A Farm Near Tifton, Georgia, C. 1930', part 1 of 'Memories of the Depression Years'.

'The Snowfall'. SA: 8; SP: 24.

'The Sometime Dancer Blues'. DJ: 81; NS: 125; OH: 62. One of two poems published elsewhere under the group title 'Two Blues'.

'The Stray Dog by the Summerhouse'. BH: 25-26; SA: 42-43; SP: 12.

'The Success'. DE: 21; SP: 79.

'The Suicides'. SP: 39-40; DJ: 64-65. Published elsewhere as 'For the Suicides' and For the Suicides of 1962'.

'The Summer Anniversaries'. SP: 114; NS: 29-30; OH: 11-12. The SP version of this poem is very different from the version published in NS and OH. A third version, very different from the other two, was published elsewhere as 'Anniversaries'.

'The Sunset Maker'. SM: 49-50; DJ: 110-111; NS: 172-173; OH: 95-97.

'The Telephone Booth in the Woods'. See 'Songs from the Telephone Booth in the Woods'.

'The Telephone Number of the Muse'. DE: 15; SP: 94; NS: 102; OH: 53.

'The Thin Man'. TP: [9]; NL: 39; SP: 67; DJ: 95; NS: 78.

'The Tourist from Syracuse'. NL: 55-56; SP: 55-56; DJ: 68-69; NS: 84-85: OH: 41-42.

'The Unbelieving Sailor to His Wife'. OB: 3.

'The Violent Ward'. BH: 23.

'The Voice of Col. von Stauffenberg Rising from Purgatory'. *Poetry* 117:1 (October-November 1997): 41. Published elsewhere as 'The Voice of Col. von Stauffenberg Ascending through the Smoke and Dull Flames of Purgatory'.

'The Voice of Col. von Stauffenberg Ascending through the Smoke and Dull Flames of Purgatory'. OH: 121. Published elsewhere as 'The Voice of Col. von Stauffenberg Rising from Purgatory'.

'The Wall'. DJ: 6; NS: 34; OH: 15. Published elsewhere as 'Sonnet' and 'Sonnet: The Wall'.

'"There is a gold light in certain old paintings"'. OH: 123.

'Things'. Comprising 'Stone', 'Pillow', 'Mirror', 'Wall', and 'Clock'. DE: 31.

'Thinking about the Past'. SP: 131; DJ: 36; NS: 130; OH: 67.

'Those Tropic Afternoons: Mrs. K'. See 'The Piano Teachers: A Memoir of the Thirties'.

'Three Odes'. Comprising 'Cool Dark Ode', 'Warm Flesh-Coloured Ode', and 'Pale Tepid Ode'. DE: 46-50; SP: 91-93; NS: 111-114.

'Thus'. SA: 29.

'Time and the Weather'. SP: 30; NS: 63. Published elsewhere as 'Houses' and 'Time and the Weather Wear Away'.

'Time and the Weather Wear Away'. OH: 33. Published elsewhere as 'Houses' and 'Time and the Weather'.

'To a Ten-Months' Child'. SA: 6.

'To Satan in Heaven'. SA: 49; DJ: 98; NS: 53; OH: 28. Published elsewhere as 'Prayer'.

'To the Hawks'. NL: 69-70; SP: 53-54.

'To the Unknown Authoress of a Hatbox of Old Letters Recently Sold at Auction'. NL: 14. Published elsewhere as 'To the Unknown Lady Who Wrote the Letters Found in the Hatbox'.

'To the Unknown Lady Who Wrote the Letters Found in the Hatbox'. NL: 14; SP: 42; DJ: 20; NS: 64. Published elsewhere as 'To the Unknown Authoress of a Hatbox of Old Letters Recently Sold at Auction'.

'To Waken a Small Person'. NL: 27; SP: 69.

'Tomorrow Is Not Yet'. Translation of 'Demain est pas encore ...' by Henri Michaux. With Dori Katz. Eds. Alexander Aspel and Donald Justice. *Contemporary French Poetry: Fourteen Witnesses of Man's Fate*. Ann Arbor, Michigan: University of Michigan Press, 1965: 45.

'Train'. See 'My South'.

'Tremayne'. Comprising 'The Mild Despair of Tremayne', 'The Contentment of Tremayne', 'The Insomnia of Tremayne' and 'Tremayne Autumnal'. *Tremayne: Four Poems by Donald Justice*: 7-10; DJ: 40-43; NS: 162-164; OH: 90-93.

'Tremayne Autumnal'. See 'Tremayne'.

'Twenty Questions'. DE: 16.

'Two Blues'. Comprising 'The Sometime Dancer Blues' and 'Angel Death Blues'. SP: 122-123.

'Two Small Vices Beginning with the Letter "L"'. Comprising 'Lethargy' and 'Luxury'. SP: 75-76.

'Two Songs from "Don Juan in Hell"'. Comprising 'Sganarelle's Song', 'Don Juan's Song'. SP: 113.

'Unflushed Urinals'. SP: 126; NS: 126; OH: 63.

'Vague Memory from Childhood'. NS: 10; OH: 102.

'Variations'. *Solo* 4 (2001): 85.

'Variations for Two Pianos'. NL: 25; SP: 34; DJ: 51; NS: 70; OH: 35.

'Variations on a Text by Vallejo'. DE: 36-37; SP: 101; DJ: 87; NS: 105; OH: 54-55.

'Variations on a Theme from James'. SA: 30-31.

'Villa Rose: A Narrative Fragment'. BH: 41.
'Villanelle at Sundown'. SM: 20; DJ: 52; NS: 155; OH: 87.
'Waiting Room'. See 'Elsewheres'.
'Wall'. See 'Things'.
'Warm Flesh-Coloured Ode'. See 'Three Odes'.
'What Alcestis Said'. OB: 9; BH: 6.
'White Notes'. DE: 18-19; SP: 95-96.
'Winter Landscape'. BH: 14.
'Wishes'. Translation of 'Deseos' by Carlos Pellicer. Ed. Mark Strand. *New Poetry of Mexico*. New York: E.P. Dutton, 1970: 173.
'Women in Love'. BH: 9; SA: 35; SP: 5; DJ: 50; NS: 46; OH: 50.
'Young Girls Growing Up (1911)'. SM: 10; DJ: 86; NS: 144.

PROSE

FICTION

'Death, Night, Etc'. *The Yale Review* 86:2 (April 1998): 63-75.
'Little Elegy for Cello and Piano'. SM: 51-55.
'The Artificial Moonlight'. SM: 57-72.
'The Lady'. *Western Review* 14:2 (Winter 1950): 127-140.
'Vineland's Burning'. *Western Review* 17:3 (Spring 1953): 203-209.

MEMOIR

'Piano Lessons: Notes on a Provincial Culture'. SM: 33-42. A revised version was published in *A Donald Justice Reader*: 115-124.

CRITICISM

DJ = A DONALD JUSTICE READER (1991)
O = OBLIVION (1998)
PS = PLATONIC SCRIPTS (1984)

'A Certain Unreasonableness of Feeling: Philip Larkin's "Coming"'. O: 111-115.
'A Great Master Obscured by History: Yvor Winters'. O: 95-100. [See under REVIEWS below.]
'Appreciation'. Eds. Orin-E Cassill, and Curt Johnson. *R.V. Cassill*. Chicago: December, 1981: 45-47.
'Baudelaire: The Question of His Sincerity; or Variations on Several Texts by Eliot'. PS: 147-151; O: 1-4.
'Benign Obscurity'. O: 80-91.
'Bus Stop: Or, Fear and Loneliness on Potrero Hill'. PS: 210-216.
'How it Began: A Postscript on Weldon Kees'. O: 103-105.

'Metres and Memory'. PS: 168-175; DJ: 149-155; O: 5-12.
'Notes of an Outsider'. O: 119-125.
'Notes on "Variations on Southern Themes"'. PS: 217-225.
'O Clouds All Afternoon Becalmed and Pure'. O: 126-135.
'Oblivion: Variations on a Theme'. O: 52-68.
'Of the Music of Poetry'. O: 69-79.
'On Purity of Style: W.C. Williams'. PS: 205-209; O: 106-110.
'On the Appreciation of Poetry'. Ed. Paul Engle. On Creative Writing. New York: E.P.
     Dutton, 1964: 127-162.
'On Writing "First Death"'. PS: 161-167.
'The Free-Verse Line in Stevens'. PS: 176-204; O: 13-38.
'The Invention of Free Verse'. DJ: 156-159; O: 39-42.
'The Poet and the Academy'. Symposium – Literature and the Academy: In Honour of the
     Inauguration of Glenn Leggett as Eighth President of Grinnell College. Grinnell, Iowa:
     The College, [1966].
'The Private History of a Poem'. PS: 152-160.
'The Prose Sublime: or, The Deep Sense of Things Belonging Together, Inexplicably'. DJ:
     160-168; O: 43-51.
'The Quiet Voice of Weldon Kees and a Postscript'. O: 101-103.
The Fugitive-Agrarian Myth. Thesis (M.A.). Chapel Hill, Norh Carolina: University of North
     Carolina at Chapel Hill, 1947.

Excerpts from Notebooks

In The Poet's Notebook: Excerpts from the Notebooks of 26 American Poets. Eds. Stephen
     Kuusisto, Deborah Tall, David Weiss. New York: W.W. Norton, 1995: 110-120.
'1980 – December 12'. Seneca Review 21:2 (1991): 95.
'Notes of an Outsider'. O: 119-125.
'"O Clouds All Afternoon Becalmed and Pure"'. O: 126-135.

Edited Works

Contemporary French Poetry: Fourteen Witnesses of Man's Fate. With Alexander Aspel.
     Includes 'A Note on the Translations' by DJ. Ann Arbor, Michigan: University of
     Michigan Press, 1965.
Midland: The Writing Workshops of the State University of Iowa. With Paul Engle and
     Henri Coulette. New York: Random House, 1961.
Syracuse Poems 1968. With a foreword by DJ. Syracuse, New York: Syracuse University
     Department of English, 1968.
The Collected Poems of Henri Coulette. With Robert Mezey. Introduction by DJ and Rob-
     ert Mezey. Fayetteville, Arkansas: University of Arkansas Press, 1990.
The Collected Poems of Raeburn Miller. CD-ROM. With Cooper R. Mackin and Richard
     D. Olson. Akron, Ohio: University of Akron Press, 1997.
The Collected Poems of Weldon Kees. Revised edition, with a new preface by DJ. Lincoln,
     Nebraska: University of Nebraska Press, 1975.
The Collected Poems of Weldon Kees. With a preface by DJ. Iowa City, Iowa: Stone Wall
     Press, 1960.
The Comma After Love: Selected Poems of Raeburn Miller. With Cooper R. Mackin and

Richard D. Olson. With a preface by DJ, Cooper R. Mackin and Richard D. Olson, and an introduction by DJ. Akron, Ohio: University of Akron Press, 1994.

The Last Nostalgia: Poems, 1982-1990. By Joe Bolton. With an introduction and a note on the text by DJ. Fayetteville, Arkansas: University of Arkansas Press, 1999.

'Unpublished Notebooks'. By Henri Coulette. With an introduction by DJ and Robert Mezey. *Common Knowledge*, 1:1 (1992): 173-185.

West of Boston. Iowa City, Iowa: The Qara Press, 1959.

INTRODUCTIONS, PREFACES, AFTERWORDS
(Unless listed under other headings))

The Torrent and The Night Before. By Edwin Arlington Robinson. A facsimile edition after 100 years of Robinson's first book. With an afterword by DJ. Maine: Gardiner, 1996.

MUSICAL SCORES

'Winesburg'. *Euphony* 1:2 (2001): 6-10.

TEXTS FOR MUSIC

'The Conspirators Make Their Vows'. Excerpt from the libretto by Donald Justice for *The Death of Lincoln. Michigan Quarterly Review* 27 (Fall 1988): 586-93.

The Death of Lincoln: A Documentary Opera. By Edwin London. Libretto by Donald Justice. Austin, Texas: W. Thomas Taylor, 1988.

The Iron Hand: An Oratorio. By Edwin London. On a text by Donald Justice, 1975.

The Seven Last Days. By Edward Miller. Text written by Donald Justice. 1971. Copy held in Box 6, Folder F231 of the Special Collections Department of the University of Delaware [See The Justice Archives below].

The Seven Last Days: For SATB Chorus, Percussion, 2 Stereo Tape Playback Systems, and 16 mm. Silent Film. By Edward Miller. Text by Donald Justice. Film by Abbott Meader. E.C.S. Mixed Media Series. Boston: Ione Press, 1971.

The Young God – a Vaudeville. By Edward Miller. Libretto by Donald Justice. Opera Department, Hartt College of Music, University of Hartford, 1969. Copy held in Box 6, Folder F231 of the Special Collections Department of the University of Delaware [see The Justice Archives below].

SOUND RECORDINGS

Betty Adcock and Donald Justice Reading their Poems. Recorded March 21, 1989, in the

Coolidge Auditorium at the Library of Congress. Archive of Recorded Poetry and Literature, Library of Congress.

Childhood and Other Poems. Washington, D.C.: Watershed Tapes, 1984.

Donald Justice Reading at Cleveland State University. Cleveland, Ohio: CSU Poetry Center, 1984.

Donald Justice Reading his Poems with Comment at Radio Station WSUI, State University of Iowa, May 1, 1958. Archive of Recorded Poetry and Literature, Library of Congress.

Donald Justice. Academy of American Poets. New York: Academy of American Poets, 1982.

Donald Justice. New Letters on the Air radio program. Kansas City, Missouri: New Letters, 1980.

Donald Rodney Justice and Carolyn Kizer Reading and Discussing their Poems in Coolidge Auditorium, April 16, 1973. Archive of Recorded Poetry and Literature, Library of Congress.

Eavan Boland and Donald Justice Reading their Poems. Recorder October 15, 1992, in the Mumford Room at the Library of Congress. Archive of Recorded Poetry and Literature, Library of Congress.

REVIEWS

'A Great Master Obscured by History'. [Review of Yvor Winters.] *Western Review* 28:2 (Winter 1954): 167-171; reprinted in O: 95-100. [See under CRITICISM, above].

'A Housman Centennial'. [Review of A.E. Housman.] *Poetry* 96:1 (April 1960): 44-47.

'Occasional Poetry'. [Review of Paul Goodman.] *Poetry* 59:2 (November 1956): 120-122.

'Sacred and Secular'. [Review of Howard Moss, Kathleen Raine and Thomas Merton.] *Poetry* 91:1 (October 1957): 41-44.

'San Francisco and Palo Alto'. [Review of Allen Ginsberg, Kenneth Patchen, Donald Drummond, Edgard Bowers, Donald Hall.] *Western Review* 22:3 (Spring 1958): 231-234.

'The Poems of J.V. Cunningham'. [Review of J.V. Cunningham.] *Poetry* 97:3 (December 1960): 181-185.

'The Unhappy Fate of the "Poetic"'. [Review of Tennessee Williams]. *Poetry* 93:6 (March 1959): 402-404.

INTERVIEWS

Clark, Geoffrey, Robert Crotty, and Robert L. McRoberts. 'An Interview with Geoffrey Clark, Robert Crotty, and Robert L. McRoberts'. *Seneca Review* 2:1 (April 1971); reprinted in PS: 15-22.

Dodd, Wayne and Stanley Plumley. 'The Effacement of Self: An Interview with Donald Justice'. *Ohio Review* 16:3 (1975): 40-63; reprinted as 'An Interview with Wayne Dodd and Stanley Plumly' in PS: 28-57.

Fitz Gerald, Gregory and William Heyen. 'An Interview with Gregory Fitz Gerald and William Heyen'. *Prairie Schooner* 47:4 (Winter 1973-1974); reprinted in PS: 23-27.

Gerber, Philip L., and Robert J. Gemmett. '"Falling Into Place": A Conversation with Donald Justice'. *Prairie Schooner* 47 (1973): 317-24.

Gioia, Dana. 'An Interview with Donald Justice'. *American Poetry Review* 25:1 (January-February 1996); reprinted in Eds. Dana Gioia and William Logan. *Certain Solitudes: On the Poetry of Donald Justice*. Fayetteville, Arkansas: The University of Arkansas Press, 1997. 171-201.

Hamilton, David and Lowell Edwin Folsom. 'An Interview with David Hamilton and Lowell Edwin Folsom'. *Iowa Review* 11: 2-3 (Spring-Summer 1980); reprinted in PS: 85-112.

Levis, Larry. 'An Interview with Larry Levis'. *Missouri Review* 4:1 (Fall 1980); reprinted in PS: 63-84.

Lofsness, Cynthia and Kathy Otto. 'An Interview with Cynthia Lofsness and Kathy Otto'. *Plaintiff* (Spring 1966); reprinted in PS: 3-14.

Ruffin, Paul. 'An Interview with Paul Ruffin'. *Sam Houston Literary Review* 3:1 (April 1978); reprinted in PS: 58-62.

Walsh, William. 'An Interview with Donald Justice'. *Chattahoochee Review* 9:4 (Summer 1989): 77-96.

ILLUSTRATIONS

Banjo Dog: Poems and Linocut Illustrations by Donald Justice. Riverside, California: Thaumatrope Press, 1995.

Jazz for Kirby. By Richard Frost. Linocut illustrations by Donald Justice. Brockport, New York: State Street Press, 1990.

Mangrove, 4:1 (1997). The issue features seven linocuts by DJ: 'The Thirties: Café', 'The Thirties: Street Band', 'Small Town', 'The Thirties: Pay Day', 'Flagler Street', 'Two Writers', and 'Bread Loaf'.

NS. Front cover illustrated with 'Courtyard at the Biltmore, Coral Gables'. (Acrylic on canvas).

OH. Front Cover illustrated with 'Orpheus Hesitated Beside the Black River' (pastel).

SM. Front cover illustrated with 'Tea Dance at the Nautilus Hotel, 1925' (coloured ink drawing).

Soho 4 (2001). Front cover illustrated with 'Lawn Party' (pastel); back cover illustrated with 'Café Café' (charcoal and watercolour).

The Ballad of Charles Starkweather. Title page illustrated with an ink drawing. West Chester, Philadelphia: Aralia Press, 1997.

The Iowa Review, 26:1 (1996). Front cover illustrated with 'Back Street, Boston, Georgia' (acrylic on cardboard). Scene misidentified in magazine as Miami, Florida.

The Iowa Review, 26:2 (1996). Front cover illustrated with 'Trains at Dusk' (pastel); back cover illustrated with 'Payday' (linocut).

The Iowa Review, 26:3 (1996). Front cover illustrated with 'Old Building, Galesburg, Illinois' (acrylic on canvas).

Secondary Works

Books

Gioia, Dana, and William Logan, eds. *Certain Solitudes: On the Poetry of Donald Justice.* Fayetteville, Arkansas: The University of Arkansas Press, 1997.

Essays, Articles, Tributes, Memoirs

CS = *Certain Solitudes*

Anonymous. 'TABA and Pulitzer prizes awarded'. *Wilson Library Bulletin* 54 (June 1980): 619.

Barker, Jonathan. Ed. Thomas Riggs. *Contemporary Poets*, 6th ed. New York: St. James Press, 1996: 560-561.

Bawer, Bruce. '"Avec une élégance grave et lente": The Poetry of Donald Justice'. *Verse* 8:3 & 9:1 (Winter/Spring 1992): 44-49; reprinted in CS: 7-17.

Bawer, Bruce. 'The Poetry in Things Past and Passing'. *Washington Post Book World* (January 3, 1988).

Bell, Marvin. 'Florida'. Poem. *Verse* 8:3 & 9:1 (Winter/Spring 1992): 35.

Benet's Reader's Encyclopedia of American Literature, 1991. 551.

Booth, Philip. 'Syracuse Years: 1966-1970'. CS: 141-146.

Bowers, Edgar. 'With Don and Jean Justice at Chapel Hill'. CS: 127-128.

Bruns, Gerald L. 'Anapostrophe: Rhetorical Meditations upon Donald Justice's "Poem"'. *Missouri Review* 4:1 (Fall 1980): 71-76.

Bynner, Witter. 'A Note on Donald Justice'. *Poetry* 97:1 (October 1960): 50.

Cobb, Jeffrey. See Peich, Michael, and Jeffrey Cobb.

Coulette, Henri. 'Tea Dance at the Nautilus Hotel (1925)'. Poem. On a painting by Donald Justice. *Verse* 8:3 & 9:1 (Winter/Spring 1992): 33.

De Jong, Mary Gosselink. '"Musical Possibilities": Music, Memory, and Composition in the Poetry of Donald Justice'. *Concerning Poetry*, 18: 1-2, (1985): 57-66.

De Jong, Mary. 'Donald Justice'. Ed. Magill. *Critical Survey of Poetry: English Language Series: Authors, Hoo-McK*, Vol. 4. Englewood Cliffs, New Jersey: Salem Press, 1982: 1528-1534.

Disch, Tom. 'An Expression of Faith'. Poem. *Verse* 8:3 & 9:1 (Winter/Spring 1992): 36.

Dobyns, Stephen. *Best Words, Best Order*. New York: St Martin's Griffin, 1996: 126-128.

'Donald Justice: A Chronology'. CS: xxiii-xxvii.

Donovan, Laurence. 'Donald Justice's Miami'. *Verse* 8:3 & 9:1 (Winter/Spring 1992): 4-8; reprinted in CS: 103-110.

Ehrenpreis, Irvin. 'Boysenberry Sherbert'. *New York Review of Books*, 22 (October 16, 1975): 3-4.

Frost, Carol. 'The Poet's Tact, and a Necessary Tactlessness'. *New England Review* 20:3 (Summer 1999): 196-204.

Fussell, Paul. *Poetic Metre and Poetic Form*. New York: Random House, 1965: 193-198.

Gioia, Dana. 'Three Poets in Mid Career'. *Southern Review* 17 (1981): 667-674.

Gioia, Dana. 'Tradition and an Individual Talent'. *Verse* 8:3 & vol. 9:1 (Winter/Spring 1992): 50-58; reprinted in CS: 67-83.

Gioia, Dana, and William Logan. Introduction. CS: xvii-xx.
Gioia, Dana, and William Logan. Introduction. Donald Justice Special Feature. *Verse* 8:3 & 9:1 (Winter/Spring 1992): 3.
Gioia, Dana, and William Logan. 'Introduction to the Critical Heritage'. CS: 205-207.
Graham, Jorie. 'Iowa City, 1976'. *Verse* 8:3 & 9:1 (Winter/Spring 1992): 20-21; reprinted in CS: 151-153.
Grimshaw, James A. Jr. 'Donald Justice'. Eds. Bain, Robert, and Joseph M. Flora. *Contemporary Poets, Dramatists, Essayists, and Novelists of the South: A Bio-Bibliographical Sourcebook.* Westport, Connecticut: Greenwood Press, 1994: 260-269.
Hoffman, Daniel. 'Poetry: Dissidents from Schools'. In *Harvard Guide to Contemporary American Writing.* Ed. Daniel Hoffman. Cambridge, Massachussetts: Harvard University Press/Belknap Press, 1979: 564-606.
Howard, Richard. 'As the Butterfly Longs for the Cocoon or the Looping Net'. Howard, Richard. *Alone with America: Essays on the Art of Poetry in the United States Since 1950.* New York: Atheneum, 1969; reprinted in CS: 53-66.
Jarman, Mark. 'Ironic Elegies: The Poetry of Donald Justice'. *Pequod: A Journal of Contemporary Literature and Literary Criticism* 16-17 (1984): 104-109.
— 'In Memory of Orpheus: Three Elegies by Donald Justice'. *Eclectic Literary Forum* 8:2 (Summer 1998): 38-43; reprinted in Mark Jarman. *The Secret of Poetry.* Ashland, Oregon: Story Line Press, 2001. 83-92.
Justus, James H. 'Donald Justice'. Eds. Robert Bain, Joseph M. Flora and Louis D. Rubin, Jr. *Southern Writers: A Biographical Dictionary.* Baton Rouge, Louisiana: Louisiana State University Press, 1979: 257-258.
— 'Poets after Midcentury'. Eds. Louis D. Rubin, Jr., Blyden Jackson, Rayburn S. Moore, Lewis P. Simpson and Thomas Daniel Young. *The History of Southern Literature.* Baton Rouge, Louisiana: Louisiana State University Press, 1985: 535-555.
Kazin, Cathrael. 'Donald Justice'. Eds. Mary Bruccoli and Jean W. Ross. *Dictionary of Literary Biography Yearbook.* Detroit, Michigan: Gale Research, 1984: 266-271.
Kinzie, Mary. 'My South: On the Porch'. Mary Kinzie. *A Poet's Guide to Poetry.* Chicago: University of Chicago Press, 1999: 349-350.
Lamorte, Pat. 'The "Ancient Rules" – A Vanishing Species?' *Georgia Review* 27:4 (Winter 1973): 499-500.
Logan, William. 'The Present Bought on the Terms of the Past'. *Crazyhorse* 20 (Spring 1980): 65-70; reprinted in CS: 270-275; reprinted again in William Logan, *All the Rage.* Ann Arbor, Michigan: University of Michigan Press, 1998: 30-35.
— 'The Force of Nostalgia', *Verse* 8:3 & 9:1 (Winter/Spring 1992): 59-66; reprinted as 'The Midnight of Nostalgia' in CS: 85-100; reprinted again in William Logan, *Reputations of the Tongue.* Gainesville, Florida: University Press of Florida, 1999: 153-167.
— 'Justice in Florida'. CS: 163-168.
London, Edwin. 'Justice and *The Death of Lincoln'.* CS: 147-150.
Martin, Walter. 'Arts of Departure'. CS: 37-52.
McCoy, James A. '"Black Flowers, Black Flowers": Meta-Criticism in Donald Justice's "Bus Stop"'. *Notes on Contemporary Literature* 26:5 (November 1996): 9-10.
McCrea, Brian. '"It Figured": Donald Justice at the Racetrack'. CS: 155-161.
McKnight, Natalie. 'Donald Justice'. Eds. Walton Beacham, Erica Dickson, and Charles J. Moseley. *Research Guide to Biography and Criticism* 5 & 6. Washington, D.C.: Beacham, 1991: 433-37.
Mezey, Robert. 'Of Donald Justice's Ear'. *Verse* 8:3 & 9:1 (Winter/Spring 1992): 37-38; reprinted in CS: 3-6.
— 'Tea Dance at the Nautilus Hotel (1925)', Poem. On a painting by Donald Justice. *Verse* 8:3 & 9:1 (Winter/Spring 1992): 34.

Morrow, Mark. *Images of the Southern Writer*. Photos by Mark Morrow. Georgia: University of Georgia Press, 1985.

Peich, Michael. 'Donald Justice: A Fine-Press Checklist'. *Verse* 8:3 & 9:1 (Winter/Spring 1992): 67-70.

Perkins, David. *A History of Modern Poetry: Modernism and After*. Cambridge. Massachussetts: Harvard University Press/Belknap Press, 1987.

Peters, Robert. 'The Child in the House'. *American Book Review* 4: 2 (January-February 1982); reprinted in Robert Peters, *The Great American Poetry Bake-Off*, Second Series. Metuchen, New Jersey, and London: The Scarecrow Press, 1982: 63-68.

Prunty, Wyatt. *Fallen from the Symboled World*. Oxford: Oxford University Press, 1990: 71-76, 208-217.

–   'At Home and Abroad: Southern Poets with Passports and Memory'. *Southern Review* 30 (Autumn 1994): 745-50.

Ramsey, Paul. 'Donald Justice as Metrist'. *Verse* 8:3 & 9:1 (Winter/Spring 1992): 39-43.

Rewa, Michael. '"Rich Echoes Reverberating": The Power of Poetic Convention'. *Modern Language Studies* 9:1 (1978-79): 25-32.

Richter, Curt. *A Portrait of Southern Writers*. Baton Rouge: Louisiana: Louisiana State University Press, 2000.

Rifenburgh, Daniel. 'Donald Justice Before a Soft-Drink Vending Machine'. Poem. *New Republic* 206:11 (March 16, 1992): 36(1).

Ritchie, Michael Karl. *From Translation to Mistranslation (Marianne Moore, Robert Bly, Ezra Pound, Louis Zukofsky, Donald Justice, Robert Lowell)*. Dissertation. Bowling Green State University, 1986.

Ross, Jean. 'Graduate School: The Thin Young Man'. *Verse* 8:3 & 9:1 (Winter/Spring 1992): 9-13; reprinted in CS: 117-126.

Ryan, Michael. 'Flaubert in Florida'. *New England Review and Bread Loaf Quarterly* 7:2 (Winter 1984): 218-232; reprinted in CS: 19-36.

St John, David. 'Scripts and Water, Rules and Riches'. *Antioch-Review* 43:3. (1985): 309-319.

Sheridan, Michael. 'The Poetry of Donald Justice, Gentleman'. *New Letters* 48:1 (Fall 1981): 114-116.

Simon, Greg. '"My Still to Be Escaped from": The Intentions of Invisible Forms – A Review of Donald Justice's *Departures*'. *American Poetry Review* 5:2 (1976): 30.

Snodgrass, W. D. 'Justice as Classmate'. *Verse* 8:3 & 9:1 (Winter/Spring 1992): 14-15; reprinted in CS: 129-132.

Stern, Richard. 'A Very Few Memories of Don Justice'. CS: 111-116.

Strand, Mark. 'A Reminiscence'. *Verse* 8:3 & 9:1 (Winter/Spring 1992): 16-17; reprinted in CS: 133-135.

Swiss, Thomas. 'The Principle of Apprenticeship: Donald Justice's Poetry'. *Modern Poetry Studies*, 10:1 (1980): 44-58.

Turco, Lewis. 'The Progress of Donald Justice'. *Hollins Critic* 29:4 (October 1992): 1-7.

Verse 8:3 & 9:1 (Winter/Spring 1992). Donald Justice Special Feature. Guest editors: Dana Gioia and William Logan.

Voigt, Ellen Bryant. 'Narrative and Lyric: Structural Corruption'. *The Southern Review* 30:4 (Autumn 1994): 725(16).

Walker, Bruce. Ed. Roger Matuz. *Contemporary Southern Writers*. Detroit, Michigan: St. James Press, 1999: 214-215.

Watkins, Clive. 'Some Reflections on Donald Justice's Poem "After a Phrase Abandoned by Wallace Stevens"'. *Wallace Stevens Journal: A Publication of the Wallace Stevens Society* 17:2 (Fall 1993): 236-44.

Wright, Charles. 'Jump Hog or Die'. *Verse* 8:3 & 9:1 (Winter/Spring 1992): 18-19; reprinted in CS: 137-140.

–   'Homage to the Thin Man'. *Southern Review* 30:4 (Autumn 1994): 741(4).

Young, David. 'Donald Justice'. Eds. Friebert, Stuart and David Young. *The Longman Anthol-*

ogy of *Contemporary American Poetry, 1950-1980.* New York and London: Longman, 1983: 218-220. An introduction to the Justice poems in this anthology.

Young, Vernon. 'Two Hedgehogs and a Fox'. *Parnassus: Poetry in Review* 8:1 (1980): 227-37.

MUSICAL SETTINGS

Those Were the Days. By Samuel Adler. Settings of poems by Donald Justice. Carl Fischer, 1999.

Twilight Songs: A Choral Song Cycle on Poetry by Donald Justice for Choral Ensemble, Soloists and Chamber Orchestra. By Ross Patterson. Thesis (M. Music). University of Washington, 1998.

REVIEWS

THE SUMMER ANNIVERSARIES (1960)

Elliott, George P. 'Donald Justice'. *Perspective* 12:4 (Spring 1962): 173-179; reprinted in CS: 214-222.

Fraser, G.S. 'Poets from America'. *Times Literary Supplement* 3056 (September 23 1960): 617.

Galler, David. 'Four Poets'. *Sewanee Review* 69:1 (Winter 1961): 169-170; reprinted in CS: 212-213.

Gunn, Thom. *Yale Review* 49:4 (June 1960): 589-598

Nemerov, Howard. *American Scholar* 29:4 (Autumn 1960): 578; reprinted in CS: 209.

Witter, Bynner. 'A Note on Donald Justice'. *Poetry* 97:1 (October 1960): 50; reprinted in CS: 210.

NIGHT LIGHT (1967)

Conarroe, Joel O. 'Five Poets'. *Shenandoah* 18:4 (Summer1967): 87-88; reprinted in CS: 228-229.

Hunt, William. 'The Poems of Donald Justice'. *Poetry* 112:4 (July 1968): 272-273; reprinted in CS: 234-235.

McMichael, James. 'Justice'. *North American Review* 252:6 (November 1967): 39-40; reprinted in CS: 230-233.

Pawlowski, Robert. *Denver Quarterly* 2:2 (Summer 1967): 175-177; reprinted in CS: 223-226.

Pritchard, William H. 'Poetry Chronicle'. *Hudson Review* 20:2 (Summer 1967): 309-310; reprinted in CS:227.

Thwaite, Anthony. 'Leaps and Plunges'. *Times Literary Supplement* 3403 (May 18 1967): 420.

DEPARTURES (1973)

Di Prisco, Joseph. 'Departures: The Poetry of Donald Justice'. *San Francisco Review of*

Books 2:3-4 (July-August 1976): 27-28; reprinted in CS: 256-260.

Ehrenpreis, Irvin. 'Boysenberry Sherbet'. *New York Review of Books* 22:16 (October 16, 1975): 3-4; reprinted in CS: 246-248.

— [Unsigned]. 'Poetry by the Yard?' *Times Literary Supplement* 3760 (March 29, 1974): 339-340; reprinted in CS: 237-240.

Howard, Richard. 'New Work from Three Poets'. *North American Review* 259:1, (Spring 1974): 79; reprinted in CS: 241-243.

McGann, Jerome J. 'The Importance of Being Ordinary'. *Poetry* 125:1 (October 1974): 45-46; reprinted in CS: 244-245.

Simon, Greg. '"My Still to Be Escaped From": The Intentions of Invisible Forms'. *American Poetry Review* 5:2 (March-April 1976): 30-31; reprinted in CS: 249-255.

SELECTED POEMS (1979)

Bedient, Calvin. 'New Confessions'. *Sewanee Review* 88:3 (Summer 1980): 670-671.

Funsten, Kenneth. *Library Journal* 105 (March 15, 1980): 728.

Grosholz, Emily. 'Poetry Chronicle'. *Hudson Review* 33:2 (Summer 1980): 304-306; reprinted in CS: 278-279.

Logan, William. 'The Present Bought on the Terms of the Past'. Crazyhorse 20 (Spring 1980): 65-70; reprinted in CS: 270-275. See under Essays, Articles, Tributes, Memoirs.

Molesworth, Charles. 'Anniversary Portraits'. *New York Times Book Review* 85 (March 9, 1980): 8, 16; reprinted in CS: 266-269.

Pettingell, Phoebe. *New Leader* 63 (January 14, 1980): 16-17.

Ramsey, Paul. 'In Praise of Makers: American Poetry in 1979'. *Sewanee Review* 88: 4 (Fall 1980): 670-671.

Young, Vernon. From 'Two Hedgehogs and a Fox'. *Parnassus* 8:1 (Fall-Winter 1979): 234-237; reprinted in CS: 261-265; reprinted in CS: 276-277.

SELECTED POEMS (UK edition, 1980)

Anonymous. *British Book News* (September 1980): 561.

Graham, Desmond. 'Recent Poetry'. *Stand* 22:1 (1980): 73

Hollinghurst, Alan. 'Good for Nothing?' *New Statesman* 100:2579 (August 22, 1980): 18; reprinted in CS: 283.

Mahon, Derek. 'Men at Forty'. *London Review of Books* 2:16 (August 21-September 3, 1980): 22; reprinted in CS: 280-282.

Young, Alan. 'Identifying Marks'. *Times Literary Supplement* 4027 (May 30, 1980): 620.

PLATONIC SCRIPTS (1984)

St John, David. 'Scripts and Water, Rules and Riches'. *Antioch Review* 43:3 (Summer 1985): 309-319. See under Essays, Articles, Tributes, Memoirs.

Wertime, Richard. 'Poets' Prose'. *Yale Review* 74:4 (Summer 1985): 608-609; reprinted in CS: 285-287.

THE SUNSET MAKER: POEMS, STORIES, A MEMOIR (1987)

Bawer, Bruce. 'The Poetry of Things Past and Passing'. *Washington Post Book World* (January 3, 1988): 4; reprinted in CS: 291-294.

Collier, Michael. *Partisan Review* 55:3 (Summer 1988): 490(2).
Donovan, Lawrence. 'Review'. *South Florida Poetry Review* 5:2 (Winter 1988): 49-51; 295-297.
Hartnett, David. 'Mythical Childhoods'. *Times Literary Supplement* 4437 (April 15-21, 1988): 420; reprinted in CS: 299-300.
Hirsch, Edward. 'Heroes and Villanelles'. *New York Times Book Review* 92 (August 23, 1987): 20; reprinted in CS: 289-290.
Howard Ben. *Poetry* 154:6 (September 1989): 342(4).
Kelly, Conor. *In Dublin* (January 7 1988).
Lucas, John. From 'Best Rhymes with Zest'. *New Statesman* 115:2976 (April 8, 1988): 28; reprinted in CS: 298.
McKee, Louis. *Library Journal* 112 (May 1, 1987): 71(1).
St John, David. 'Memory As Melody'. *Antioch Review* 46 (Winter 1988): 102-9; reprinted in David St John. *Where the Angels Come Toward Us*. Fredonia, New York: White Pine Press, 1995: 120-128.
Yenser, Stephen. *Yale Review* 77:1 (Autumn 1987): 124-133.

A DONALD JUSTICE READER: SELECTED POETRY AND PROSE (1991)

Gioia, Dana. 'A Poet's Poet'. *New Criterion* 10:9 (May 1992): 68-71; reprinted in CS: 301-305.
Kirby, David. 'Refined Craftsman'. *American Book Review* 15:1 (April-May 1993): 26; reprinted in CS: 3-6-311.
Lynch, Doris. *Library Journal* 116:21 (December 1991): 144-145.
Monaghan, Pat. *Booklist* 88:9 (January 1, 1992): 805-806.
Richman, Robert. 'Intimations of Inadequacy'. *Poetry* 162:3 (June 1993): 160-166; reprinted in CS: 312-319.
Stefanile, Felix. *Christian Science Monitor* 84:101 (April 20, 1992): 13

NEW AND SELECTED POEMS (1995)

Anonymous. *Virginia Quarterly Review* 72:2 (1996): S64.
Anonymous. 'Take it from the Masters'. *Economist* (March 13 1999): Review, 14.
Boening, John. *World Literature Today* 72:2 (Spring 1998): 379-380.
Cook, Eleanor. *Partisan Review* 64:4 (Fall 1997): 671-673.
Foy, John. *Parnassus: Poetry in Review* 23:1-2 (Spring/Summer 1998): 287-293.
Haines, John. 'Poetry Chronicle'. *Hudson Review* 50 (Summer 1997): 320-1.
Hofmann, Michael. *New York Times Book Review* (December 10, 1995): 13.
Kitchen, Judith. *Georgia Review* 50:2 (Summer 1996): 386-388.
Leithauser, Brad. 'Getting Things Right'. *New York Review of Books* 43:14 (September 19, 1996): 49-51.
McCorkle, James. *Kenyon Review* 19:3-4 (Summer-Fall 1997): 180-188.
Murphy, Bruce. *Poetry* 168:3 (June 1996): 168-171.
Anonymous. *Publishers Weekly* 242:35 (August 28, 1995): 108.
Ratner, Rochelle. *Library Journal* 120:15 (September 15, 1995): 72-73.
Rector, Liam. *Ploughshares* 21:4 (Winter 1995): 209-212.
Seaman, Donna. *Booklist* 92:2 (September 15, 1995): 132.
Shoaf, Diann Blakely. *Antioch Review* 54:3 (Summer 1996): 377-378.

Spiegelman, Willard. 'Poetry in Review'. *Yale Review* 84 (April 1996): 160-83.
Strand, Mark. *New Yorker* 71:36 (November 13, 1995): 124-126.

THE ACADEMY OF AMERICAN POETS ARCHIVE: DONALD JUSTICE (sound recording)

Speirs, Gilmany. *Booklist* 94:4 (October 15, 1997): 422.

OBLIVION: ON WRITERS AND WRITING (1998)

Anonymous. *Publishers Weekly* 245:23 (June 8, 1998): 57(1).
Barton, Emily. *New York Times Book Review* 103 (July 19, 1998): 19.
Harp, Jerry. 'Fidelities to Form'. *Iowa Review* 29:3 (Winter 1999): 167 +.
Thompson, N.S. 'Orpheus Hesitated Beside the Black River, Poems, 1952-1997'. *Times Literary Supplement* 5026 (July 30, 1999): 23.
Wiman, C. *Poetry* 174:5 (1999): 286-297.

ORPHEUS HESITATED BESIDE THE BLACK RIVER (1998)

Anonymous. 'Poetry in Brief'. *Independent on Sunday* (March 14 1999): Culture, 13.
Barker, Sebastian. *PN Review* 127 (1999): 64.
Thompson, N.S. 'Orpheus Hesitated Beside the Black River, Poems, 1952-1997'. *Times Literary Supplement* 5026 (July 30, 1999): 23(1).

BIBLIOGRAPHIES

Peich, Michael, and Jeffrey Cobb. 'Donald Justice: A Bibliographical Checklist'. CS: 323-330.

THE JUSTICE ARCHIVES

Donald Justice's papers are held by the Special Collections Department in the University of Delaware Library, Newark, Delaware 19717-5267, USA (Tel: +001 302 831 2229; e-mail: askspec@hawkins.lib.udel.edu). The holding comprises ten linear feet of material dating from 1936, and is stored under Manuscript Collection Number 191. A detailed list of contents, running to more than forty pages, is to be found on the library's website, at:

http://www.lib.udel.edu/spec/findaids/justice/

The archive is open for research.

THE CRITICS

'Donald Justice seems to this reviewer to have as fine an ear for language as any young poet writing.'

– Karl Shapiro, 1958

'Donald Justice is a discovery of welcome importance in his *The Summer Anniversaries*, a 1959 Lamont Poetry Selection, and the judges who found him should be happy.

What matter that he is two persons, one assuredly a poet, the other – at least for me – not ...'

– Witter Bynner, review of *The Summer Anniversaries*, 1960

'Mr Justice has less humour and range than Mr Starbuck, but a finer ear for poise, balance and climax, and a more unified sense of style.'

– G.S. Fraser, review of *The Summer Anniversaries*, 1960

'Donald Justice's book appears in the excellent series from Wesleyan University Press. There are one or two obvious misfires in it (the only disastrous one being the final poem, which is really too close to Auden to be taken seriously), but otherwise it is a most accomplished collection. There is a great deal to be thankful for in such poets as ... Donald Justice. Their very modesty is part of their virtue. They are humble before the tangible world, attempting to understand it at the same time as they reproduce it. It is a brave humility, too, much braver than the desire to do away with the rules of common sense and perception so that the idiosyncrasies of one's personality may rule the page, much braver than the arrogant cultivation of an individual voice at the expense of everything else ... We have here some very distinguished writing.'

– Thom Gunn, review of *The Summer Anniversaries*, 1960

'Mr Justice is an accomplished writer, whose skill is consistently subordinated to an attitude at once serious and unpretentious. Although his manner is not yet fully disengaged from that of certain modern masters, whom he occasionally echoes, his own way of doing things does in general come through, a voice distinct although very quiet, in poems that are delicate and brave among their nostalgias. Of several whose melancholy lucidity moved me and will remain in memory, I mention especially "Beyond the Hunting Woods".'

– Howard Nemerov, review of *The Summer Anniversaries,* 1960

'Page after page of surprisingly unassimilated rhetoric owing to others prevents these poems from having at least the virtues of imitations.'

– David Galler, review of *The Summer Anniversaries,* 1961

'Mr Justice is ... a good craftsman. He fulfils the formal requirements of the son-net, the villanelle, and the sestina with aplomb, and varies the forms suitably whenever his needs are stronger than the forms'. He moves easily from one metre to another. He understands what a line can do and his lines do it. He employs rhyme, off-rhyme, stanza, alliteration, refrain, prayer, suppressed narra-tive, irony, wordplay with grace and an almost flawless control. Why is such skill an occasion for anything less than admiration?

...
The charge that Mr Justice is derivative can be supported only by a reader with a tin ear. To be sure, one can find Yeats, Auden, Eliot and Ransom in his poetry – also "This little Pig Went to Market". Most of the craft of poetry is taking in techniques, rhythms, tones of the other poets and making them one's own. To hear Mr Justice's poetry as artful pastiche of others is not to catch his voice.'

– George P. Elliott, review of *The Summer Anniversaries,* 1962

'Justice brings a controlled, urbane intensity to his Chekhovian descriptions of loss and of the unlived life, of the solitary, empty, "sad" world of those who receive no mail, have no urgent hungers – who, in short, lead their lives but do not own them.'

– Joel O. Connaroe, review of *Night Light,* 1967

'Whenever Donald Justice's poetry is mentioned, many people who should know something about poetry say, "Justice? Oh yes; a good technician but terribly limited." The tone of their comments more often than not suggests that technical skill is something to be avoided by poets or, at best, hardly necessary to the writing of good poetry. Just as peculiar is the kind of answer they give if pressed for explanations of "limited". It turns out they don't mean range of subject, for they agree Justice has a wide range of subject; they don't mean acuity – "ex-tremely perceptive and intelligent," they say of Justice. Do they mean then he is sensitive to a fault? Perhaps too delicate or quiet? No, they do not mean that because such judgments are often only a matter of taste. Do they mean he lacks the huffings and puffings of James Dickey, the pitying self-indulgence of Anne Sexton, the rhetorical *weltschmertz* of Robert Lowell, the density of John Berryman, or ..., and the conversation usually breaks off.

...

Donald Justice is, I think, a good poet who is as interested in life, death, hate, love, fun, and sorrow as anyone; however, I think he is more interested in how these matters receive their expression than many other poets are.'

– Robert Pawlowski, review of *Night Light*, 1967

'Donald Justice is witty, gentle, sophisticated, a quiet recorder of the pathetic and inconsequential. The poems of *Night Light* are undemanding notations; and if they get no louder applause than that, it is because they do not seem to expect it.'

– Anthony Thwaite, review of *Night Light*, 1967

'To account for the insistent reticence of this poet, for what he himself, in a characteristic oxymoron, calls "the major resolution of the minor", we must a little recuperate the blurred meaning of elegance – a term very promiscuously accorded these days and very precariously worn – from the original sense of the term itself: a consistent choice of words and their arrangement in the exemplification of a single taste. An American impulse, as it were: from many, one. At the age of forty, Donald Justice had not produced, or at least had not ventured to publish, so many poems, perhaps three dozen in his first book, *The Summer Anniversaries* (which was the Lamont Poetry Selection for 1959), and a dozen more in *A Local Storm*, three years later. To pursue the patriotic figure, about as many poems as there are States in the Union. But he has written enough – as there are States enough – for us to collect from the whole sum and tenor of his discourse, as Berkeley would say, a provisional perspective, and the winnowed singleness of that perspective, the unmistakable and unmistaken unity of an artistic identity, is proof, then, of his elegance, a reminder too that the word "glamour", a cheaper sister of elegance in misuse, is merely a Scots corruption of the word "grammar".

– Richard Howard, 'As the Butterfly Longs for the Cocoon
or the Looping Net', 1971

'Mr Justice writes only about what he can ennoble through language. People who fascinate him are elegiacally evoked by a handful of quiet images, and made fascinating to us. The poet conveys these remarkably suggestive images through

121

a select troupe of words varied and repeated in a sustained, low-keyed music. While sounding casual, the repetitions mark rhythmic patterns and bring out ambiguities that secretly reflect a central idea. In a still subtler motion the poet shifts from third person to second, or from apostrophizing an absent hearer to addressing himself. These shifts give one a sense of suddenly coming close to a beauty that had seemed far off.

To move us, images must be sharp, fresh, precise. To move us permanently, to be worth memorizing, they must not be narrowly bound in time or place. Listeners of many ages, many cities, must recognize them. Only a gifted poet can invent such images; if the large themes of love, heroism and death are to be handled, only a profoundly gifted poet will discover images that are not second-hand. Mr Justice has this power.'

– Irvin Ehrenpreis, review of Departures, 1974

'[S]ome of the most assured, elegant and heartbreaking – not broken, but breaking – verse in our literature so far.'

– Richard Howard, review of Departures, 1974

'Donald Justice ... is an aesthete in the mould of Rossetti. *Departures,* like his earlier books, is filled with Rossettian apparatus: mirrors, hypnagogic landscapes, poems about poetry and a life in art ... Justice by now knows his poetic self so well that he seems incapable of self-deception. Many of his best poems emerge as nostalgic interior landscapes – empty, silent, and moving to a slow-motion clock. But, again like Rossetti, Justice recognizes that this is not an analytic but an erotic and performative personality. His interior poems are not confessions, or acts of questing and discovery; they are abstract maps offered to the reader, who is placed, momentarily, in a landscape of such purity and stillness that he is forcibly returned to an awareness of the importance of primitive resources.'

Jerome J. McGann, review of Departures, 1974

'For the last twenty years or so, while several other poets have acquired the major prizes and been honoured (or broken) by national attention, Donald Justice, in comparative obscurity, has written the finest poems recently published in this country. His book, *Departures,* is an altogether brilliantly achieved book deserving of much wider critical interest and acclaim than so far has come its way.

Perhaps his obscurity is a function of the nature of his vision. The poems refuse to advertise themselves or their maker, and perhaps Justice's meticulous care, his absolute refusal to strike the fashionable pose, his unwillingness to work for the easy effect, his strong and quiet confidence – are ultimately accountable for his obscurity, but at the same time accountable for that alluring and suggestive quality which radiates within his work.'

— Joseph Di Prisco, review of *Departures*, 1976

'When poets have grown complete in whatever apprenticeship they may have chosen, and are ready to say what they must say: there are no visible forms that can hold them. This holds true all the way back to Milton, who wrote the first "free verse", and it is intoxicating to see Justice now unfettered by the forms that circumscribed and dictated the action in his early poems; and to see him working with sources that are not only energetic and new, but demanding in conception and daring in stance.'

— Greg Simon, review of *Departures*, 1976

'I doubt if there are six poems in this selection which could be claimed for the public sensibility. But Justice has written a dozen lyrics I'd call virtually incomparable – of a kind rivalled only by W.S. Merwin or the early Merrill. And it's my sad duty to acknowledge that most were written fifteen or twenty years ago. Justice has lacked the gift for renewing himself poetically; however, the initial gift remains sufficiently impressive to inhibit critical approaches.'

— Vernon Young, review of *Selected Poems*, 1979

'"First Death", "The Summer Anniversaries", "The Suicides", and still other poems are admirable, but the collection as a whole reflects an uncertain talent that has not been turned to much account.'

— Calvin Bedient, review of *Selected Poems*, 1980

'Donald Justice's *Selected Poems* play variations on the themes of time's passage, mortality, afternoon and autumn. His writing never succumbs to the black despair which corroded the poetry of Weldon Kees (whom he served so well as editor), but is held by a kind of mental equipoise and illusionless wit. I would say that any young American poet must come to Donald Justice's work sooner or later to learn the state of his art ...'

— Emily Grosholz, review of *Selected Poems*, 1980

'Many admiring poets and a few perceptive critics have paid careful, even studious attention to Donald Justice's poetic skill, which seems able to accomplish anything with an ease that would be almost swagger if it were not so modest of intention. He is, among other things, the supreme heir of Wallace Stevens. His brilliance is never at the service merely of flash and display; it is always subservient to experienced truth, to accuracy, to Justice, the ancient virtue as well as the personal signature. He is one of our finest poets.'

— Anthony Hecht, 1980

'Donald Justice's poems ... persistently haunt and are haunted by the past, to the extent that their present is characterized by a weary passivity, a lack of vitality that is supported by fastidious formal elegance ... The poems occupy a cultured space, as aware of European poetry as of American (though in a way typical too of the British awareness of American poetry, that of a couple of generations earlier) – but with a certain lassitude and narcissism, looking in the mirror as much as out of the window. Formal but *fatigués,* they create the impression of getting great job-satisfaction without actually doing much work. It is unfair but true to say that the beautiful printing and production of the book increase this sense of artistic complacency which further reduces the emotional pressure of the work.'

— Alan Hollingshurst, review of *Selected Poems,* 1980

'Justice's is a poetry of loss; to thwart that loss he attempts to solidify the world of his past in his poems, a private archaeology preserving what otherwise would vanish. His achievement has been to write ever more cunningly of a poet's central concerns: his loss in time, his imaginative gain – the present bought on the terms of the past. Only the spareness of his output and his characteristic self-abnegation have denied him a more general recognition.'

— William Logan, review of *Selected Poems,* 1980

'This is a varied and marvellously accomplished volume, and if it seems a little short on ambition – there is no major attempt at a comprehensive statement – at least he knows what he can and cannot do. Measuring the successes against the failures in these 130-plus pages, one is left in no doubt that here is a very fine poet indeed, and one who, on this side of the Atlantic at least, has yet to receive the attention he deserves.'

— Derek Mahon, review of *Selected Poems,* 1980

'The publication of Donald Justice's *Selected Poems* is an occasion for gladness and gratitude, for seeing the old and new poems together, a good company.
Tone is his mastery, the quality by which style lets us know how to take what

is said in the astute and many modes of fashioning the true.

"On a Painting by Patient B of the Independence State Hospital for the Insane" is an array of diverse and effortlessly compatible styles, at a little distance remarking, keeping near. "Counting the Mad" is one of the great parodies of the language, a counting rhyme for a child turned into something as plainspoken as horror can tell. "Anthony Street" describes a place, at morning then at evening, clearly, in detail, mostly literally. The composed order intensifies the seeing of the disorderly, inconcluded, harmed. "The headlights, turning, grope their way".

"Bus Stop" is sparer of resource and even more foreboding of presence. "Twenty Questions" invents from an old game a new mode. "Incident in a Rose Garden" is a story, a dialogue, a reversal, as medieval as modern as true.

His comic poems are also a treat of many-shapedness: the long leisurely descriptiveness of "Anonymous Drawing" with the sufficient exclusiveness of its end, the honed instancy of "Horizon", the perched littleness of "Little Elegy", the internal and measured dialogue of "Heart", the inventively varied "Variations for Two Pianos", the elusive briefness of "Lethargy".

The elegiac, shifting, many-shaded, often lyric, often darkened, is in my judgement the best and most central mode. "Early Poems" complains, amusedly and tenderly, that the speaker's early poems were "fashionably sad", and moves on to some unfashionable clarity of sadness.

The truth is, though, that the later poems are more inclined to fashion, to randomness as partial method, to fragmentation, to deconstructive poetics, to wandered and incompleted narrative. Yet his poetic integrity, a guardian and kindly Muse, bears Justice safely by such swamps and murmured gleams. His fragments sound completed, his notes "From a Notebook" nicely compose. His gift for order is an irresistible gift.

The elegiac appears in a number of his poems, including some already mentioned. One may add "Landscape with Little Figures" ("It's winter, it's after supper, it's goodbye"), "The Snowfall", "Memories of the Depression Years", the magnificent "Absences".

And, returning over and over to my mind, "An Elegy Is Preparing Itself".

> There are pines that are tall enough
> Already. In the distance,
> The whining of saws; and needles,
> Silently slipping through the chosen cloth.
> The stone, then as now, unfelt,
> Perfectly weightless. And certain words,
> That will come together to mourn,
> Waiting, in their dark clothes, apart.'

– Paul Ramsey, review of Selected Poems, 1980

'Damn that Donald Justice, anyway! He's written all the good lines!'

– Lilly Berry, in John Irving's novel, The Hotel New Hampshire, 1981

'Justice has come to be recognized not only as one of America's most elegant and distinctive contemporary poets but also as one of its most significant.'

– Cathrael Kazin, 1983

'In his fifth collection of poems, *The Sunset Maker*, Donald Justice establishes himself as an elegiac poet of the first order. He may be, concomitantly, the resident genius of nostalgia in the ever-expanding house of American poetry. Mr Justice is a scrupulous tactician of melancholy and loss who approaches his subjects with what one of his poems calls "a love that masquerades as pure technique". His temperament is wryly romantic – as he puts it in "Villanelle at Sundown", "One can like anything that diminishment has sharpened" – but his style is firmly classical. His new book is a little anthology of the strictest traditional forms, including a few slyly complicated nonce forms of his own devising. If, as Ezra Pound once said, "technique is the test of a man's sincerity," Mr Justice is surely one of the sincerest poets working today.'

– Edward Hirsch, review of *The Sunset Maker*, 1987

'On the whole, *The Sunset Maker* is a deeply affecting volume – a beautiful, powerful meditation by a modern master upon the themes of aging, lost innocence, and the unalterable, terrifying pastness of the past.'

– Bruce Bawer, review of *The Sunset Maker*, 1988

'Donald Justice has always been a poet for whom memory and art are manifestations of the same haunting. Like his contemporaries Anthony Hecht and James Merrill, he has remained faithful to the Stevensian notion of a "supreme Fiction" while avoiding the more extreme cerebralism of Stevens's own poetry. The mood of *The Sunset Maker,* his fourth collection, is characteristically elegiac; but nostalgia and sadness are constantly being filtered through an almost buoyant sense of creative renewal.'

– David Hartnett, review of *The Sunset Maker*, 1988

'[I]n the avoidance of extremes, in the mild and musical manner with which he treats his quiet despair, [Justice] has managed to write poems which are, to use his own adjectives, sad, regretful and complete.'

– Conor Kelly, review of *The Sunset Maker*, 1988

'[Donald Justice's] new collection *The Sunset Maker* amounts to not much more than sonorous whinging. Yes, he is immensely skilled, but why so many dying falls, why the darkness without extended wings? One way of answering this question is to point out that Justice is in thrall to a particularly damaging convention of American letters which takes melancholy as a synonym for cultural fastidiousness.

... [W]hat Justice lacks is that "thunder" without which saying "no" becomes little more than a self-pitying refusal to rejoice.'

– John Lucas, review of *The Sunset Maker*, 1988

'Justice is the poet of a world in which loss is ubiquitous, sorrow inevitable, and adult joy always bittersweet, a world in which the genuinely heroic act, for a literary artist, is not to thrash about uncontrollably, raising a manic and ugly din, but to fashion a body of work whose beauty and poise and gravity in the face of life's abomination may, one trusts, help it to endure.'

– Bruce Bawer, '"Avec une Elégance Grave et Lente":
the Poetry of Donald Justice', 1992

'[Donald Justice] is our most notable "poet's poet", with all the ambiguities that bittersweet honorific implies. He has won most of the major awards – the Lamont, the Pulitzer, the Bollingen. His work appears in all the anthologies edited by poets, but it remains conspicuously absent in most of those compiled by professors. He is widely regarded as the most influential poetry-writing teacher now alive. His former students from Iowa, Syracuse, Gainesville, and Bread Loaf constitute a Who's Who of American poetry. They include writers in every aesthetic camp. Since his didactic emphasis has been on craft, concentration, and precision, he has founded no school of poetry. Consequently, his work has attracted almost no attention from academic critics. Yet he is one of the few living writers whose verses American poets are likely to quote from memory.

...

... The seventy-six poems gathered in *A Donald Justice Reader* constitute an encyclopaedia of literary form and style. It is remarkable enough to find sonnets, villanelles, couplets, and sestinas coexisting in the same volume as surreal odes and aleatory "sonatinas" – not to mention poems based on blues lyrics and nursery rhymes. But surely it is unique to find all these styles handled with equal mastery, to see the same author use such apparently contradictory procedures to produce convincing poems. Whereas another writer might have borrowed an unfamiliar style to try something different in a new poem, Justice somehow managed to reinvent each manner from within. He created poems that were both strikingly different and yet recognizably his own.

...

... *A Donald Justice Reader* ends with fifty-odd pages of prose – a memoir of childhood piano lessons in Depression-era Miami, two short stories, and three brief literary essays. I knew all these pieces previously, but, rereading them with the special savour for design and detail that a second or third viewing allows, I felt a keen and unexpected disappointment. I wasn't disappointed with the selections. No, every one was perfect of its kind. My chagrin was with Justice. Why had someone this good written so little prose.

... Anyone who worries that enduring poems are no longer being written should read this singularly impressive collection.'

– Dana Gioia, review of *A Donald Justice Reader*, 1992

'The method of Donald Justice's later poetry accepts nostalgia, a nostalgia with little of the emotional consolation of submission and more of the religious desolation of confession. In his arching dark ironies, Justice has long proved an irritant to the simpler taxonomies of American poetry, which find it convenient to ignore whatever lies beyond the margin of immediate comprehension. Justice almost never uses the self as the location of drama, for the great tragedy moving through the little event. In his detachment he is a modern (his most obvious forebears Williams and Stevens) at a time when the sharper reliefs of Modernism have been eroded.

...

The past is a series of half-forgotten particulars; but in Justice's poetry, to what I think is an unusual degree, the observer stands aside from the force of the particulars, not immune to them (because continually establishing relations between them) but curiously detached from their access. It is as if a poet were permitted every intimacy with a speaker except intimacy itself; that is, all the stoic intimacies of knowledge but few of feeling. This may seem the reverse of what we expect when the speaker is the poet ...

The inadequacy of contemporary poetry may lie in its confidence of feeling (even its representation of feeling) and its absence of a knowledge susceptible to anything outside feeling. The determinism of contemporary poetry demands that feelings be enactments of events, perhaps better the performatives of events; that is why the past in most poems is so often on trial. One of the merits of Justice's poetry lies, not in its absence of emotion, but in its withholding of confidence from emotion. The events that suffer this withholding are permitted a range of insinuation more disturbing because less mediated. At a felt distance, the past can't be revealed or re-enacted, only rendered (for this reason Justice's exclamations, his mark of exhausted plangency, seems twice lonely). Such a speaker is unreliable because he will not accede to the conventions of sentiment.'

– William Logan, 'The Midnight of Nostalgia', 1992

'This is state-of-the-art, as they say. I wish it were truly representative of the state of the art. But, still, it gives some cheer to remember that at the end of the twentieth century, when American poetry is drearier and more amateurish than it has been at any time since the end of the nineteenth, a few writers are "saying the thing once for all and perfectly." The gratitude I feel for "Last Evening" and for so many of Donald Justice's poems is the gratitude I feel for any act or gesture of love and loving care. That is, no doubt, "a love that masquerades as pure technique." But it *is* love.'

— Robert Mezey, 'Of Donald Justice's Ear', 1992

'Justice likes to remind readers of the distance between poetry and life. One way he does this is to write artificially — to use metres. "Like the moustaches and baggy pants of the old comedians," Justice writes in the essay "Metres and Memory", metres "put us on notice that we are at a certain distance from the normal rules and expectations of life." Another way to point out the poem's distance from reality is to divulge its literary origins. One more way to show how far poems are from life is to use imagery that suggests it. Justice isn't above a flagrantly self-reflexive remark, like "the *the* has become an *a*" (in "Homage to Wallace Stevens"). Usually, though, Justice's poems live a double life — as a commentary on life, and as a commentary on the poem's status as a nettlesome aesthetic object.'

— Robert Richman, review of *A Donald Justice Reader*, 1993

'The complexities of language have always been tempting to fakes; but while using fully the complexities of his language, Donald Justice has always demonstrated that the highest purpose of literature is to illuminate those things which are hard, disturbing, painful, moving, and repeat themselves — not to obscure them.'

— John Irving, 1995

'This stirring volume replaces Justice's *Selected Poems* (1980) and includes poems drawn from six earlier collections ... but its crowning glory is a wealth of beautiful new work.'

— Donna Seaman, review of *New and Selected Poems*, 1995

'Donald Justice's *New and Selected Poems* enacts a brilliant accommodation to almost everyone's expectations of poetry. The poems have a sweet and measured gravity that engages us on a level more profound than the one we usually find ourselves on ... Reading Justice, one feels keenly that a poem is an act of retrieval — that, as it memorializes, so it revives ... Memory and rapture are so closely intertwined that they become a single gesture of sustained regard.'

— Mark Strand, review of *New and Selected Poems*, 1995

'His career has never been marred by an insincere or bogus stretch; there is no phase of his you'd wish he hadn't included. And the 'new' in this volume are poems as rewarding as anything he has done ... For decades now, Justice has sought to capture the quality of the far-flung, subsiding sunlight, and the best of his poems should – like chased metal in a museum case – hold their gleam for a long while.'

– Brad Leithauser, review of *New and Selected Poems*, 1996

'There is not a poem in this nimbly-turned collection which does not vibrate with a quiet, decent music. He is both traditional and self-reliant. If Homer and Dante are determinants, so are Wordsworth, Rimbaud, Hart Crane, Henry James, and especially Rilke. He has a passing resemblance to X.J. Kennedy. His collection closes with an account of work which "will be seen as strong and clean and good." That is exactly the impression his poetry makes on the reader.
...
... He is a true poet of the Parnassian order, gifted with realism, delicacy, irony, and lyricism.'

– Sebastian Barker, review of *Orpheus Hesitated by the Black River*, 1998

'[O]ne of our most lucid and visible poets ... [A]n intelligent and highly intelligible work.'

– Emily Barton, review of *Oblivion*, 1998

'Justice belongs to the well-made-poem generation that ruled America in the Fifties, and his own poems are very well made indeed, roughed up a little with the inflections of the living voice ... Good stuff, human through and through.'

– Anonymous review of *Orpheus Hesitated by the Black River*, 1999

'Justice's always accomplished work has ... gained in power and expression with each one of his collections since *The Summer Anniversaries* ...
If he is an Orpheus who could be said to have hesitated, he has done so not from any Prufrockian fear, but in order to meditate deeply on his life and times ...
In a short preface to *Oblivion: On Writers and Writing*, the poet informs the reader that poets of his generation "did not get much into the habit of criticism," and further states that he is perhaps the only one who regrets the fact. Given the quality and lucidity of these essays, it is a regret many can share.'

– N.S. Thompson, review of *Orpheus Hesitated Beside the Black River*
and *Oblivion*, 1999